Contents

CW00687428

Stingers!
The F/A-18 Hornet
Backbone of the Navy's Carrier Strike Force

The F/A-18 Hornet is both a single and two-seat, twin-engine, multi-mission fighter/attack aircraft originally designed for the US Navy and Marine Corps to operate from either aircraft carriers or land bases. The F/A-18 fills a variety of roles such as air superiority, fighter escort, suppression of enemy air defences, reconnaissance, forward air control, close and deep air support, and day and night strike missions, and is able, by literally the flick of a switch to go from air defence to ground attack in the same mission. The F/A-18 Hornet has now replaced the F-4 Phantom, A-7 Corsair, A-6 Intruder and the mighty Tomcat in Navy and Marine service and a new version the EA-18 will replace the EA-6B Prowler in the near future. The Hornet's digital flight control system provides excellent handling qualities, allowing pilots to fly the airplane with relative ease and at the same time, gives the aircraft exceptional manoeuvrability and permits the pilot to concentrate on operating the weapons system. A solid thrust-to-weight ratio and superior turn characteristics permits the F/A-18 to hold its own against any adversary and gives it the power to maintain evasive actions, and although a lack of range was perhaps the aircraft's biggest drawback, this problem was addressed in later versions.

The men and their machines, as a pair of VFA-106 Hornets head over the skies of Bosnia

F/A-18A/B 'Legacy' Hornet

While the general configuration of the YF-17 prototype was retained, the F-18 became a completely new airplane. To meet the single-place fighter and attack mission capability, full use was made of new technology with digital computers coupled with cathode ray tubes for the cockpit displays and appropriate pilot control configurations were based on extensive evaluations in simulators.

During development, two-seat trainer versions were added, to be built in limited numbers as TF/A-18s, intermingled with the basic single-seat versions. Minimum changes were made to incorporate the second cockpit, with the two-seat airplanes retaining the ability to perform combat missions. Making the first flight in November 1978, the F/A-18A and its two-place derivative, later redesignated the F/A-18B, underwent most of their development testing at the Naval Air Test Centre under the new single-site testing concept. The original F/A-18A and F/A-18B became operational in 1983 replacing Navy and Marine Corps F-4s and A-7s. It quickly became the battle group commander's mainstay because of its capability, versatility, availability, whilst reliability and ease of maintenance were emphasised in its design. Thus the F/A-18s have consistently flown three times more hours without failure than other Navy tactical aircraft, while requiring half the maintenance time.

Libyan Raiders
F/A-18A's in 'Operation Prairie Fire' and 'Eldorado Canyon'

During early 1986 four F/A-18A Hornet Squadrons were deployed aboard the USS Coral Sea: two Navy units, VFA-131 and VFA-132 and two Marine Corps units VMFA-314 and VMFA-323, flying as part of CVW-13 for what was expected to be a routine deployment to the Atlantic and the Mediterranean. However, the United States were at that time concerned that Libya's Colonel Khaddafi had become an important source of support for anti-US terrorist activity in Europe. In addition, Khaddafi claimed the Gulf of Sidra as Libyan territorial waters, declaring a 'Line of Death' across the entrance to the Gulf beyond which ships of other nations would not be allowed to enter. In response, President Reagan ordered the Sixth Fleet to begin 'Freedom of Navigation' manoeuvres in the Gulf of Sidra to demonstrate American resolve to operate freely in what it believed to be international waters and the F/A-18s from the Coral Sea flew combat air patrols, protecting the carrier group from any Libyan aircraft. The Hornets were frequently called upon to intercept and challenge numerous MiG-23s, MiG-25s, Su-22s, and Mirages sent out by Libya to harass the fleet. The Hornets often flew within a few feet from their Libyan counterparts, fully armed ready to shoot if needed.

In Operation 'Prairie Fire' in March 1986, the same Hornets went into direct action for the first time, flying several air strikes against Libyan shore installations that were harassing the US fleet. Flying in bad weather and at wave top heights carrying both Shrike and HARM anti-radar missiles the F/A-18s attacked the SA-5 missile site

at Sirte which had been painting US aircraft on its radars. This was the combat debut for the Hornet, and also marked the first combat use of the AGM-88A HARM anti-radar missile. All involved Hornets returned to their carriers without mishap.

Following further prevarication by the Libyan Government, on April 15 1986, Operation 'Eldorado Canyon' was staged. This was a combined USAF/Navy attack on targets in and around Tripoli and Benghazi. For the USAF this involved UK based F-111 strike aircraft and for the Navy and Marines it marked another milestone for the new Hornets - their task was again defence suppression, firing both Shrike and HARM missiles at radar targets. Once more the Hornets acquitted themselves well and had begun to gain respect amongst commanders

F/A-18C/D Hornet

Following a successful run of more than 400 A and B models, the US Navy began taking deliveries of improved F/A-18C (single-seat) and F/A-18D (two-seat) models in September 1987. These Hornets carried AMRAAM Advanced Medium Range Air-to-Air Missiles and the infrared imaging Maverick air-to-ground missile. Two years later, the C/D models came with improved night attack capabilities and these additional components included a navigation forward looking infrared (NAVFLIR) pod, a raster head-up display, night vision goggles, special cockpit lighting compatible with the night vision devices, a digital colour moving map and an independent multipurpose colour display.

F/A-18Cs came with synthetic aperture ground mapping radar with Doppler beam sharpening mode to generate ground maps and this capability permitted crews to locate and attack targets in adverse weather and poor visibility or to precisely update the aircraft's location relative to targets during the approach, a capability that improved bombing accuracy. New production F/A-18Cs received the APG-73 radar upgrade radars starting in 1994, providing more precise and clear radar displays.

The F/A-18C Night Attack Hornet had a pod-mounted Hughes AN/AAR-50 thermal imaging navigation set, a Loral AN/AAS-38 Nite Hawk FLIR targeting pod, and GEC Cat's Eyes pilot's night vision goggles, whilst a few F/A-18D two-seat Hornets were configured as the F/A-18D ATARS reconnaissance version, with an under nose

A brace of 'Death Rattlers' from the US Marines during 'Desert Storm'

One of the 'Golden Dragons' of VFA-192 prepares to take on fuel during a patrol over Iraq

5

A pair of F/A-18D's from the US Marine Corps VMFA(AW)-121 taxi out for an armed patrol over Iraq

pallet-mounted electro-optical suite comprising a blister-mounted IR Linescan and two roll-stabilized sensor units.

Desert Storm Stingers

During the Gulf War of 1991, some 190 US Navy and Marine Corps Hornets were used in the action, 106 on aircraft carriers and eighty-four with land-based Marine Corps units. One was lost in combat, F/A-18C 163484 and its VFA-81 pilot Lieutenant Commander Michael Speicher were lost to ground fire (some sources say this plane was shot down by missiles fired by an Iraqi MiG-25 that was in the area), and two were lost in non-combat accidents. Three more were hit by infrared-homing surface-to-air missiles, but were able to made it back to be repaired and used again, demonstrating the essential robustness of the airframe. The Hornets flew six types of missions: fleet air defence, SEAD interdiction, self-escort, offensive and defensive counter-air, and close support. On a typical SEAD mission, the Hornet carried two drop tanks, two AGM-88A HARM missiles, two AIM-7 Sparrow missiles, and two AIM-9 Sidewinder missiles. On interdiction missions, they would typically carry three Mk.20 Rockeye cluster bomb units, two drop tanks, two AIM-7s and two AIM-9s. In attacks on Silkworm anti-ship missile sites, the Hornets used AGM-142 Walleyes, SLAM (Standoff Land Attack Missile, a ground attack version of the AGM-84 Harpoon anti-ship missile), and Mk.80 iron bombs. Two US Navy F/A-18Cs scored air-to-air kills during the war when on the first day of the war four

Hornets from VFA-81 Sunliners were on their way to a ground target when two of them were engaged by Iraqi F-7As (Chinese-built MiG-21). Lieutenant Commander Ed Fox in F/A-18C 163508 and Lieutenant Nick Mongillo in F/A-18C 163502 immediately switched from air-to-ground to air-to-air modes and bagged a MiG apiece with AIM-9 Sidewinder shots without having to first dump their bombs, and then pressed on to their targets.

Operation 'Deny Flight' Bosnia Peace Keepers

No sooner had the first Gulf War ended than another conflict, this time in Europe, erupted over Bosnia, and again both Navy and Marine Corps Hornets were thrust into a peace-keeping role. The US Marine Corps 'blooded' their latest asset the F/A-18D two-seat multi-role Stinger in the skies above the beleaguered countries taking part in operation 'Deliberate Force' and 'Deny Flight'. Flying out of Aviano AB the 'swing-role' F/A-18D Hornets arrived with their APG-73 radars and F404-GE-402 engines, laser designators and uprated defensive systems. The aircraft flew with a true mixed bag of weaponry with AIM-7, AIM-120 and AIM-9 air-to-air missiles; laser guided or iron bombs, HARM and Maverick missiles. Many operations were anti-radar SEAD missions and because of the close proximity of targets to populated areas the use of precision guided munitions in these tasks was paramount. Also because poor weather conditions prevented the safe use of LGBs in daylight, at least half of the Hornets' missions were flown at night.

25% larger wing area, and carry 33% more internal fuel which will effectively increase mission range by 41% and endurance by 50% and also incorporates two additional weapon stations. This allows for increased payload flexibility by mixing and matching air-to-air and/or air-to-ground ordnance.

Firepower for the Super Hornet can be dangled from eleven weapon stations with two more wing stations than the F-18C/D and these can support a full range of armaments, including: AIM-9 Sidewinder, AIM-7 Sparrow and AIM-120 AMRAAM air-to-air missiles; guided air-to-ground weapons such as Harpoon, SLAM, GBU-10, HARM and Maverick; and free-fall air-to-ground bombs such as Mk.76, BDU-48,Mk.82LD, Mk.82HD and Mk.84. The aircraft can also carry the GPS/ inertial guided joint direct attack munitions (JDAM) and joint stand-off weapon (JSOW). The F/A-18E and F also have a new lightweight gun system in the shape of the General Dynamics M61A2, which has a firing rate of 7,200 shots per minute and a linkless ammunition feed system. The AN/ASQ-228 ATFLIR (Advanced Targeting Forward Looking Infra-Red) is the main electro-optical sensor and laser designator pod for the Super Hornet. Defensive systems are coordinated through the Integrated Defensive Countermeasures system IDECM which provides co-ordinated situation awareness and manages the countermeasures, the

The pilot pays close attention as the aircraft is settles onto the 'cat track'

Operation 'Iraqi Freedom'

The F/A-18s had continued to be employed in operations over Iraq in the years following the first Gulf War in various roles as part of Operations Northern and Southern Watch, and they were again thrust into action in 2003 during the second Gulf War 'Operation Iraqi Freedom'. In some quarters the Hornets soon became known as the 'Universal Soldiers' of both the Navy and Marines, and OIF saw the combat debut of the newest aircraft in the Navy's inventory the F/A-18E single-seat and F/A-18F two-seat 'Super Hornet', more of which later. The bulk of the Hornets in theatre were the older 'C' models or upgraded 'A+' versions but still hugely capable and deadly bomb-trucks or fighters, and indeed the Hornets were also called in to strafe ground targets! The US Marines brought ashore elements from VMFA(AW)-121 and 533 flying the F/A-18D, and VMFA-225, 232 and 251 to Al Jaber, flying the F/A-18C and undertaking all weather attack missions in support of coalition forces, in the same manner as those from the US Navy's Hornet units.

Enter the Super-Bug - the F/A-18E/F

The multi-mission F/A-18E/F Super Hornet strike fighter is a major upgrade of the combat-proven night strike F/A-18C/D. The Super Hornet now provides the battle group commander with a platform that has the range, endurance, and ordnance carriage capabilities comparable to the A-6 which the original Hornet replaced. The F/A-18E/F aircraft are 4.2 feet longer than earlier Hornets, have a

Full 'burners......

expendable decoys, and signal and frequency control of emissions. The IDECM system includes the ALE-47 47 threat adaptive countermeasures dispenser system capable of firing chaff, flares, and the POET and GEN-X active decoys, the ALE-50 towed decoy and the AN/ALR-67(V)3 radar warning receiver which intercepts, identifies and prioritises threat signals. The Super Hornet was originally equipped with the APG-73 however this has now been replaced by the AN/APG-79 AESA set. The Super Hornet is also outfitted for the SHARP multi-function reconnaissance pod and the Joint Helmet Mounted Cueing System. US Marine Corps aircraft are being fitted with the Northrop Grumman Litening AT Advanced Targeting pod, with FLIR, CCD TV, laser spot tracker, infrared laser marker and infrared laser rangefinder / designator.

Super Hornets at War

The first unit to bring their F/A-18 Super Hornets to combat was VFA-115 when on November 6 2002 a pair of F/A-18Es conducted a Response Option strike in support of Operation 'Southern Watch on' two SAM launchers at Al Kut and on an air defence command and control bunker at Tallil air base in Iraq. One of the pilots, Lieutenant John Turner also dropped 2,000 lb (900 kg) JDAM bombs for the first time from the F/A-18E in wartime. In support of Operation Iraqi Freedom, VFA-14, VFA-41 and VFA 115 flew CAS, strike, escort, SEAD and tanker sorties, whilst a pair F/A-18Es from VFA-14 and a pair of F/A-18Fs from VFA-41 were forward deployed to the USS Abraham Lincoln where the VFA-14 jets flew mostly as aerial refuellers and the VFA-41 jets as FAC(A)s.

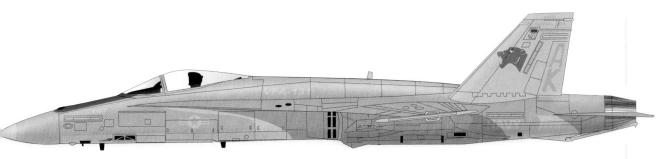

McDonnell Douglas F/A-18A Hornet of VFA-131 'Wildcats' during operation 'El Dorado Canyon'. Note the early style camouflage pattern under the LERX.

McDonnell Douglas F/A-18A Hornet of VMFA-323 'Death Rattlers' aboard the USS Coral Sea during operation 'El Dorado Canyon'

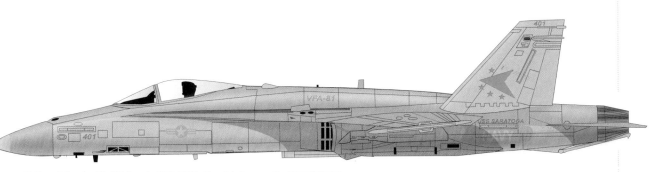

McDonnell Douglas F/A-18C Hornct of VFA-81 'Sunliners' during operation 'Desert Storm'.

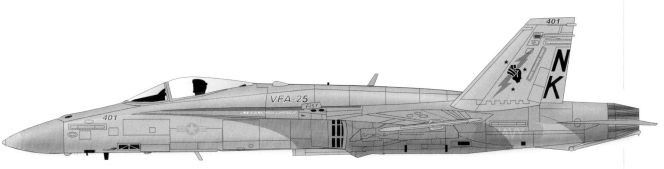

McDonnell Douglas F/A-18C Hornet of VFA-25 'Fist of the Fleet' during operation Iraqi Freedom

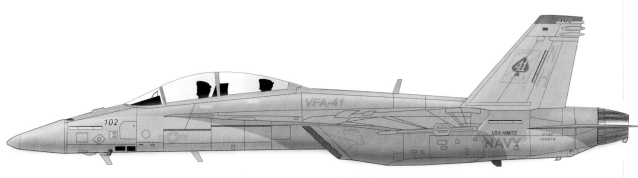

Boeing F/A-18F VFA-41 'Black Aces' aboard the USS Nimitz during operation 'Enduring Freedom'

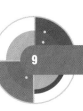

A VFA-14 F/A-18E prepares to launch for a patrol over Afghanistan

The CAG Bird from VFA-37 prepares to head for the Iraqi skies

Super Hornets from VFA-211 and VFA-136 taxi out

Home safely from a trip into Iraq in 1991

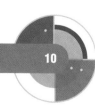

With its angular intakes and larger LERX an F/A-18F come in to land

Operation 'Enduring Freedom'

Both 'Super' and 'Legacy' Hornets remain committed to Operation 'Iraqi Freedom', and also to operations in Afghanistan where on September 8 2006 the Super Hornets dropped their first weapons, expending both GBU-12 and GBU-38 bombs against Taliban strongholds to the northwest of Kandahar. **CS**

Two of the few ATARS fitted F/A-18D reconnaissance capable Hornets

During 'Desert Storm' a Navy F/A-18C refuels from a USAF KC-135

A pair of VFA-126 'Knighthawks' on patrol

Spooks at Sea

The F-4 Phantom

Now retired, the Phantom was a mainstay on US carrier decks for many years

The McDonnell Douglas F-4 Phantom II was, and is a two-seat, twin-engined, all-weather, long-range supersonic fighter/bomber originally developed for the US Navy by the McDonnell Aircraft Company. Proving itself highly adaptable, it became a major part of the carrier air wings of the Navy and Marine Corps and later was adopted by the USAF. It was used extensively by all three of these services during the Vietnam War, serving as the principal air superiority fighter for both the Navy and Air Force, as well as being important in the ground-attack and reconnaissance roles. First entering service in 1960, the Phantom continued to form a major part of US military air power throughout the 1970s and 1980s, being gradually replaced by the F-15 Eagle, F-16 Fighting Falcon, F-14 Tomcat and F/A-18 Hornet. The Phantom was also operated by the armed forces of eleven other nations. Production ran from 1958 to 1979, with a total of 5,195 aircraft being built.

In 1953, McDonnell Aircraft began work on revising its F3H Demon, seeking expanded capabilities and better performance. The company developed several projects including a variant powered by a Wright J67 engine, and others powered by two Wright J65, or two General Electric J79 engines. On 19 September 1953, McDonnell approached the US Navy with a proposal for a 'Super Demon', and uniquely, the aircraft was to be modular – as it could be fitted with one- or two-seat noses for different missions, with different nose cones to accommodate radar, photo cameras, four 20 mm cannon, or FFAR unguided rockets in addition to the nine hardpoints under the wings and the fuselage. The Navy was sufficiently interested to order a full-scale mock-up of the F3H-G/H, but felt that the upcoming Grumman XF9F and the Vought XF8U-1 already satisfied the need for the supersonic fighter. The McDonnell design was therefore reworked into an all-weather fighter-bomber with eleven external hardpoints, and on 18 October 1954, the company received a letter of intent for two YAH-1 prototypes and on 26 May 1955, four Navy officers arrived at the McDonnell offices and, within an hour, presented the company with an entirely new set of requirements. Because the Navy already had the Skyhawk for ground attack and F-8 Crusader for dog-fighting, the project now had to fulfill the need for an all-weather fleet defence interceptor. A second crewman was added to operate the powerful radar.

The crowded deck of the USS Independence with Phantoms and Skyhawks present

The XF4H-1 was designed to carry four semi-recessed AIM-7 Sparrow radar-guided missiles, and to be powered by two J79-GE-8 engines, and as in the F-101 Voodoo these sat low in the fuselage to maximize internal fuel capacity and ingested air through fixed geometry inlets. The thin-section wing had a leading edge sweep of 45° and was equipped with a boundary layer control system for better low-speed handling. Wind tunnel testing had revealed lateral instability requiring the addition of 5° dihedral to the wings and in order to avoid redesigning the central section of the aircraft, McDonnell engineers only angled up only the outer portions of the

wings by 12°, which averaged the required 5° over the entire wingspan. The wings also received their distinctive 'dogtooth' for improved control at high angles of attack and the all moving tailplane was given 23° anhedral to improve control at high angles of attack while still keeping the tailplane clear of the engine exhaust. In addition, air intakes were equipped with movable ramps to regulate airflow to the engines at supersonic speeds. All-weather intercept capability was achieved thanks to the AN/APQ-50 radar and to accommodate carrier operations, the landing gear was designed to withstand landings with a sink rate of 23 ft/s (7 m/s), while the nose strut could extend by some 20 in (50 cm) to increase angle of attack at takeoff.

On 30 December 1960, the VF-121 'Pacemakers' became the first Phantom operator with its F4H-1Fs (F-4As) and VF-74 'Be-Devilers' became the first deployable Phantom squadron when it received its F4H-1s (F-4Bs) on 8 July 1961. The squadron completed carrier qualifications in October 1961 and Phantoms undertook first full carrier deployment between August 1962 and March 1963 aboard USS Forrestal. The second squadron to receive F-4Bs was VF-102 'Diamondbacks', who promptly took their new aircraft on a shakedown cruise aboard the USS Enterprise. VF-114 'Kittyhawks' participated in the September 1962 cruise aboard USS Kitty Hawk and by the time of the Gulf of Tonkin incident, thirteen of the thirty-one deployable Navy squadrons were armed with the type. F-4Bs from USS Constellation made the first Phantom combat sortie of the Vietnam War on 5 August 1964, flying bomber escort in Operation 'Pierce Arrow' and the first Phantom air-to-air victory of the war took place on 9 April 1965 when an F-4B from VF-96 'Fighting Falcons' shot down a Chinese MiG-17

A pair of F-4S Phantoms from VF-301 in low-vis grey colours

'Fresco'. The Phantom was then shot down, apparently by missile from one of its own wingmen! On 17 June 1965, an F-4B from VF-21 'Freelancer' piloted by Commander Louis Page and Lieutenant John C. Smith shot down the first North Vietnamese MiG of the war.

On 10 May 1972, Lieutenant Randy 'Duke' Cunningham and Lieutenant JG William P Driscoll flying an F-4J, callsign 'Showtime 100', shot down three MiG-17s to become the first aces of the war. On the return flight, the Phantom was damaged by an enemy SAM. To avoid being captured, Cunningham and Driscoll flew their burning aircraft using only the rudder and afterburner (the damage to the aircraft rendered conventional control nearly impossible), until they could eject over water. During the war, Navy Phantom squadrons participated in eighty-four combat tours with F-4Bs, F-4Js, and F-4Ns. The Navy claimed forty air-to-air victories at the cost of seventy-three Phantoms lost in combat (seven to aircraft, thirteen to SAMs and fifty-three to AAA. An additional fifty-four Phantoms were lost in accidents. By 1983, the F-4Ns had been completely replaced by F-14 Tomcats, and by 1986 the last F-4Ss were exchanged for F/A-18 Hornets, the Navy operated The F-4B, the F-4J, the F-4N (and upgraded F-4B) and the F-4S (an upgraded F-4J) versions of the naval Phantom, each progressively being uprated with new radar, ECM and avionics systems, whilst still retaining the basic airframes. On 25 March 1986, an F-4S of VF-151 Vigilantes became the last Navy Phantom to launch from an aircraft carrier, in this case, the USS Midway and on 18 October 1986, an F-4S from the VF-202 'Superheats', a Naval Reserve fighter squadron, made the last-ever Phantom carrier landing while operating aboard USS America. In 1987, the last of the Naval Reserve-operated F-4Ss were replaced by F-14As.

Everything down and ready to catch the wire

The Marines received their first F-4Bs in June 1962, with the 'Black Knights' of VMFA-314 at MCAS El Toro becoming the first operational squadron and in addition to attack variants, the Marines also operated several tactical reconnaissance RF-4Bs. Marine Phantoms from VMA-531 arrived in Vietnam on 10 April 1965, flying close air support missions from land bases. Marine F-4 pilots claimed three enemy MiGs (two while on exchange duty with the USAF) at the cost of seventy-five aircraft lost in combat, mostly to ground fire, and four in accidents. On 18 January 1992, the last Marine Phantom, an F-4S, was retired by the 'Cowboys' of VMFA-112 with the unit re-equipping with F/A-18 Hornets. ▣

The US Marines were also major Phantom users

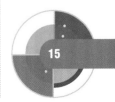

Bomb-Truck

Grumman's A-6 Intruder

All-weather strike – from Vietnam to Desert Storm

The Grumman A-6 Intruder was a twin jet-engine aircraft designed for use by the US Navy and Marine Corps as a medium attack aircraft and served between 1963 and 1997 as an all-weather replacement for the A-1 Skyraider, and the Intruder's large blunt nose and slender tail inspired a number of nicknames, including 'Double Ugly', 'The Mighty Alpha Six', 'Iron Tadpole' and 'Drumstick'. The jet nozzles were originally designed to swivel downwards for shorter take-offs and landings, but this feature was never incorporated in prototype or production aircraft. The cockpit uses an unusual double pane windscreen and side by side seating where the pilot sits in the left seat, while the Bombardier/Navigator (B/N) sits to the right. The incorporation of this additional crew member with separate responsibilities enabled low-level attacks in all weather conditions. The wing was very efficient at subsonic speeds and the aircraft was also equipped with 'deceleron' style airbrakes on the wings with two panels that opened in opposite directions; in this case, one panel goes up, while another goes down.

The Intruder was given the designation of A-6A in 1962, and entered squadron service in February 1963 becoming the Navy and Marine Corps principle medium all weather attack aircraft from the mid-1960s through the 1990s, and also served as an aerial tanker either in the dedicated KA-6D version or by use of a buddy store.

A-6 Intruders first saw action during the Vietnam War, where they were used extensively against targets 'in country'. The aircraft's long range and heavy payload coupled with its ability to fly in all weathers made it invaluable during the war. However, its typical mission profile of flying low to deliver its payload made it especially vulnerable to anti-aircraft fire, and in the eight years of operations eighty-four aircraft were lost. The first loss occurred on 14 July 1965 when an Intruder from VA-75 from the carrier USS Independence, flown by Lt Donald Boecker and Lt Donald Eaton, commenced a dive on a target near Laos. An explosion under the starboard wing damaged the starboard engine, causing the aircraft to catch fire and the hydraulics to fail. Seconds later the port engine failed, the controls froze, and the two crewmen ejected. Both crewmen survived. Of the Intruders lost to all causes during the war, ten were shot down by SAMs, two were shot down by MiGs, sixteen were lost to operational causes, and fifty-six were lost to conventional ground fire and 'Triple A'. The last Intruder to be lost during the war was from VA-35 flown by Lt's Graf and Hatfield, from the USS America; they were shot down by ground fire on 24 January 1973 while providing close air support. The airmen ejected and were rescued by a Navy helicopter. Whilst the Navy operated their A-6s from carriers most of the US Marine Corps Intruders were shore based in South Vietnam at Chu Lai and Da Nang.

A Marines A-6 from VMA(AW)-533 about to launch

A tri of A-6Es
on deck

Note the 'double-
bubble' canopy and
side-by-side seating

Coming in close
– an A-6 from
VA-52

17

Wings folded aboard the USS Midway

were used to patrol the no-fly zone in Iraq and provided air support for Marines during Operation 'Restore Hope' in Somalia, and the A-6E left Marine Corps service on 28 April 1993. The A-6 also saw further duty over Bosnia in 1994 but was by now slated for retirement, and the A-6E and KA-6D were quickly phased out of service in the mid-1990s, the last aircraft retiring in February 1997.

A-6A

The initial version of the Intruder was built around the complex and advanced DIANE (Digital Integrated Attack/Navigation Equipment), intended to provide a high degree of bombing accuracy even at night and in poor weather. DIANE consisted of multiple radar systems: the AN/APQ-92 search radar replaced the AN/APQ-88 on the YA-6A, and a separate AN/APG-46 for tracking, AN/APN-141 radar altimeter, and AN/APN-122 to provide position updates to the AN/ASN-31 INS. An air-data computer and ballistics computer integrated the radar information for the bombardier/navigator (BN) in the right-hand seat. When it worked, DIANE was perhaps the most capable nav/attack system of its era, giving the Intruder the ability to fly and fight in even very poor conditions. Total A-6A production was 488, including six pre-production prototypes. Many of the surviving aircraft were converted to other variants.

A-6B

To provide Navy squadrons with a defence suppression aircraft, a mission dubbed 'Iron Hand' in Navy parlance, nineteen A-6As were converted to A-6B standard from 1967 to 1970. The A-6B had many of its standard attack systems removed in favour of special equipment to detect and track enemy radar sites and to guide Shrike and Standard ARM anti-radar missiles, with AN/APQ-103 radar replaced earlier AN/APQ-92 in A-6A and AN/APN-153 navigational radar replaced earlier AN/APN-122 in A-6A. Five were lost in combat, and the rest were later converted to A-6E standard in the late 1970s.

A-6 Intruders were later used in support of other operations, in Lebanon in 1983, where an aircraft was downed by Syrian missiles on 4 December. Intruders also saw action in April 1986 operating from the aircraft carriers USS America and Coral Sea during the bombing of Libya during Operation 'El Dorado Canyon' when aircraft from VA-34 'Blue Blasters' and VA-55 'Warhorses' undertook strike missions. During Operation Desert Storm in 1991, Navy and Marine Corps A-6s logged more than 4,700 combat sorties, providing close air support, destroying enemy air defences, attacking Iraqi naval units, and hitting strategic targets. They were also the Navy's primary strike platform for delivering laser guided bombs, and operated from the Saratoga, John F Kennedy, Theodore Roosevelt Midway, Ranger, America, and Nimitz, while U.S. Marine Corps A-6s operated ashore, primarily from Shaikh Isa AB in Bahrain. Three A-6s were shot down in combat by SAMs and AAA. Following Desert Storm, Intruders

A quartet of Marines Intruders

Twilight Intruder.....

A-6C

Twelve A-6As were converted in 1970 to A-6C standard for night attack missions against the Ho Chi Minh Trail in Vietnam. These aircraft were fitted with a 'Trails/Roads Interdiction Multi-sensor' or TRIM pod in the fuselage as well as a 'Black Crow' engine ignition detection system.

KA-6D

In the early 1970s 78 A-6As and 12 A-6Es were converted for use as tankers to support other strike aircraft. The DIANE system was removed and an internal refuelling system was added, sometimes supplemented by a D-704 refuelling pod on the centerline pylon.

A-6E

The definitive attack version of the Intruder, introduced in 1970, with its first deployment, 9 December 1971, with vastly upgraded navigation and attack systems. The earlier separate search and track radars of the A-6A/B/C were replaced by a single AN/APQ-148 multi-mode radar, and the onboard computers with a more sophisticated IC based system, as opposed to the A-6A's DIANE discrete transistor-based technology. A new AN/ASN-92 inertial navigation system was added, along with the CAINS (Carrier Aircraft Inertial Navigation System), for greater navigation accuracy. Beginning in 1979, all A-6Es were fitted with the AN/AAS DRS - Detecting and Ranging Set, part of the 'Target Recognition and Attack Multi-Sensor' – TRAM - system, with a small, turret, mounted under the nose of the aircraft, containing a FLIR boresighted with a laser spot-tracker/designator and the TRAM was matched with a new Norden AN/APQ-156 radar. The BN could use both TRAM imagery and radar data for extremely accurate attacks, or use the TRAM sensors alone to attack without using the Intruder's radar. TRAM also allowed the Intruder to autonomously designate and drop laser guided bombs and in addition, an AMTI - Airborne Moving Target Indicator - allowed the aircraft to track a moving target (such as a tank or truck) and drop ordnance on it. A-6E models totalled 445 aircraft, about 240 of which were converted from earlier A-6A/B/C models.

An A-6E is guided onto the 'cat-track'

An A-6 at the end of Operation 'Desert Storm'

19

SLUFF - Light Strike

The A-7 Corsair II

Vought's cut-down Crusader

A brace of 'SLUFF's over the Gulf at the end of 'Desert Storm'

the initial batch of aircraft, designated 'A-7.' In 1965, the aircraft received the popular name 'Corsair II', after Vought's highly successful World War II fighter. Compared to the F-8 fighter, the A-7 had a shorter, broader fuselage and the wing had a longer span, and the unique variable incidence of the F-8 was omitted. To achieve the required range, the A-7 was powered by a Pratt and Whitney TF30-P-6 engine but without the afterburner needed for supersonic speeds. The aircraft was fitted also with an AN/APQ-116 radar, and later this was replaced the AN/APQ-126, which was integrated into the ILAAS digital navigation system. The radar also fed a digital weapons computer which made possible accurate delivery of bombs from a greater stand-off distance, greatly improving survivability compared with faster platforms. It was the first U.S. aircraft to have a modern head-up display, which showed critical information such as dive angle, airspeed, altitude, drift and aiming reticle. The integrated navigation system allowed for another innovation – the projected map display system (PMDS) which accurately portrayed the aircraft's position on two different scales.

The YA-7A made its first flight on 27 September 1965, and began to enter Navy squadron service late in 1966 and the first squadrons reached operational status on 1 February 1967, and began combat operations over Vietnam in December of that year. The A-7 required only 11.5 hours of maintenance per mission resulting in quick turnaround and high number of combat-ready aircraft. However, after several years of exposure to the harsh marine conditions aboard aircraft carriers, the maintenance

The Ling Temco Vought A-7 Corsair II or 'Sluff' (Short Little Ugly Fat Fella – in polite conversation) was carrier-based subsonic light attack aircraft introduced to replace the US Navy the A-4 Skyhawk, initially entering service during the Vietnam War. The Corsair was later adopted by the US Air Force to replace the A-1 Skyraider and F-100 Super Sabre In 1962, The US Navy began preliminary work on its 'VAX' (Heavier-than-air, Attack, Experimental) program, a replacement for the Skyhawk with greater range and payload, with particular emphasis being placed on accurate delivery of weapons. These requirements were finalized in 1963, with the 'VAL' (Heavier-than-air, Attack, Light) competition.

To minimize costs, all proposals had to be based on existing designs, and Vought, Douglas, Grumman and North American all submitted designs. The Vought proposal was based on the successful F-8 Crusader, having a similar configuration, but being shorter and stubbier, with a rounded nose. It was selected as the winner on 11 February 1964, and on 19 March the company received a contract for

hours per sortie were often twice this amount. The A-7 also offered a plethora of leading-edge avionics compared to contemporary aircraft and this included data link capabilities and fully 'hands-off' carrier landing abilities when used in conjunction with its approach power compensator (APC) or auto throttle. On 5 November 1965, the USAF announced that it too would purchase a version of the A-7, designated the 'A-7D', for use by Tactical Air and the most important difference from the Navy version was the adoption of the Allison TF41-A-1 engine, a licence-built version of British Rolls-Royce Spey. The Navy was so impressed with the performance of the USAF machines that they ordered their own version with the TF41 engine and M61 cannon, the 'A-7E'. In 1979 the first around-the-clock night-attack FLIR-capable aircraft were delivered to VA-81 at NAS Cecil Field, Florida and VA-22 at NAS Lemoore, California. These aircraft were fitted with a non-jettisonable FLIR pod on the left inboard wing station which placed images onto the pilot's HUD. In 1986, 231 A-7Es were equipped to carry the Low-Altitude Night Attack (LANA) pod, which projected amplified light image on the HUD and, in conjunction with radar, provided terrain following down to 460 mph at 200 ft.

From 1967 - 1971 a total of twenty-seven Navy squadrons took delivery of four different A-7A/B/C/E models and in 1974, when the USS Midway (CV 41) became the first Forward Deployed Naval Force (FDNF) aircraft carrier to be home-ported in Yokosuka, In 1978, these squadrons (VA-93 and VA-56) finally transitioned to the much more advanced A-7E model and six Naval Reserve squadrons would also eventually transition to the A-7. The first U.S. Navy A-7As were

An A-7E comes in to refuel during 'Desert Storm'

deployed to Vietnam in 1967 with VA-147 'Argonauts' aboard the USS Ranger and these aircraft made their first combat sortie on 4 December 1967. In the following months, VA-147 flew around 1,400 sorties losing only one aircraft. The Navy's improved A-7B model arrived in Vietnam in early 1969, with the definitive A-7E following in 1971. The 'Sidewinders' and 'Marauders' then deployed from Jun 1972 to Mar 1973 aboard USS America (CV-66) for a ten-month combat cruise and during that deployment, VA-82 played a role in the attack that destroyed the Thanh Hoa Bridge, a vital link in the North Vietnamese Army supply lines and a target that seemed

You can almost feel the tension as this A-7 prepares for launch

21

The famous 'Desert Storm Sluff' –
although it was actually painted to
celebrate the end of the conflict!

Note the large Sharksmouth on this VA-93 bird

The low-viz paintwork on the A-7 soon became discoloured and patchy

indestructible during the Vietnam War. Four A-7Cs from VA-82 successfully delivered 8,000 lb of high explosives, with two aircraft carrying a pair of 2,000 lb Walleyes, while two others carried also 2,000 lb Mk.84 bombs. In a simultaneous attack, the center piling on the bridge's west side was hit and broke the span in half and following this attack the Thanh Hoa bridge was considered permanently destroyed and removed from the target list. On 15 May 1975, A-7E aircraft aboard the USS Coral Sea provided air cover for what was considered the last battle of the Vietnam War, the recovery of the SS Mayauez after it was hijacked by Cambodian communists.

Navy A-7E squadrons VA-15 and VA-87, from the USS Independence, provided close air support during the invasion of Grenada, codenamed 'Operation Urgent Fury', in October 1983 and other Navy A-7s also provided air support during the US Mission to Lebanon in 1983. On 24 March 1986, during the Gulf of Sidra dispute with Libya and the so-called 'Line of Death', Libyan air defences fired SAM-5 missiles at two F-14s from VF-102 operating from the USS America, that were orbiting in international air space. A-7s from the USS Saratoga responded by firing the first AGM-88 HARM anti-radar missiles combat, and the following day A-7s again launched HARM missiles against other Libyan SAM sites. In April 1986, Navy Sixth Fleet A-7Es from VA-72 and VA-46 aboard USS America also participated in Operation 'El Dorado Canyon', the retaliatory attack on Libya, again firing HARM and Shrike anti-radar missiles.

In August 1990, while USAF A-7s stayed home in favour of

A brace of A-7's from VA-72. Note the FLIR pod on the rear aircraft

A-10s, the US Navy deployed two of their last A-7E squadrons as part of Operation 'Desert Shield' aboard the USS John F Kennedy, the only carrier of six deployed to Desert Storm to operate the A-7. VA-46 and VA-72 made the last combat sorties of the A-7 in flying from the Red Sea to attack targets throughout Iraq. The A-7 was used both day and night to attack a wide range of heavily defended deep interdiction targets in Iraq as well as 'kill boxes' in Kuwait, employing a variety of weapons including PGMs, such as the TV-guided Walleye glide bomb, unguided general purpose bombs, and HARM missiles. The A-7 was also used as a tanker in numerous in-flight refuelling missions. Very quickly after the end of the Gulf War the Navy retired its last 'Sluffs' and the pilots and crews were all saddened to see their faithful steed removed from the decks of US carriers. **CS**

Sunset on the 'Sluff'

Top Cat
The F-14 Tomcat
Grumman's last fighter. Best of the Best

An iconic deck-shot, typical of an F-14 launch aboard the USS Constellation

The perceived threats defined during the 1960s foresaw a cornucopia of Soviet fast flying combat aircraft carrying both cruise and anti-ship missiles capable of destroying entire battle groups at sea. The US Navy's 1959 Fleet Air Defense Fighter (FADF) requirement emphasised the need to counter this threat with the use of an airborne platform able to operate from an aircraft carrier and capable of carrying long-range missiles, each with a high degree of autonomous flight control.

The US Navy had taken a keen interest in the Douglas F6D-1 Missileer which was able to carry an advanced radar and eight huge Bendix AAM-M-10 Eagle long-range air-to-air missiles, able to take down intruders at distances of up to 110 nautical miles, before they could get close enough to be a real threat. The whole idea was to say the least a little far sighted and the Missileer concept was now becoming a lumbering missile truck that would not be capable of close-in dogfighting! Developmental problems with both the Missileer and the Eagle missiles led to both projects being cancelled

F-14 Prototype #8 with dummy Sparrow missiles. Credit: Grumman

in 1960, leaving the Navy still searching for a solution to its air defence needs.

A change of Government in 1961 saw President John F Kennedy in office and after intensive studies to select a compromise between USAF and Navy requirements, a so-called 'commonality approach' was brought into being, which was designed to save costs by building one aircraft for both services. Therefore the 'TFX' (Tactical Fighter Experimental) specification was applied to aircraft for both services and in August 1961, and in the face of fierce opposition, the TFX was imposed on the Navy and their objections overridden. Against recommendations a General Dynamics/Grumman team was awarded what was then the biggest production contract for a single aircraft type - and hence was born the F-111 Air Force/Navy fighter. The plan was for General Dynamics to build the F-111A for the Air Force and Grumman to build the F-111B for the Navy.

The Naval F-11B aircraft was nicknamed 'Sea Pig' by Navy crews and test personnel and clearly it was just not going to work and despite attempts to fix the problems, Congress cut funds in May 1968 and the program was formally axed in December, after the construction of a total of seven F-111B prototypes and evaluation aircraft. In July 1968, with the F-111B clearly dead, the Navy began a new competition for a fleet defence interceptor under their new and redefined 'VFX' program. Grumman, purveyors of fine Naval aircraft for many years had the inside track in this particular contest, and were announced as the winner on January 14, 1969 and a mock-up of their definitive swing wing Design-303 concept was inspected by Navy officials in the spring of 1969. The designation 'YF-14' was subsequently assigned to the Grumman design and they were subsequently awarded a research, development, test, and evaluation contract.

First Tomcats

From the outset the F-14 was going to be a huge aircraft with tandem seating for a pilot in front and radar intercept officer (RIO) in back sitting on Martin-Baker GRU-7A ejection seats. The cockpit layouts were specialised for both crew, with little duplication and the F-14's sophisticated yet simple integrated control system was unlike

Getting the huge Tomcat back on deck!

A trio of F-14As from the Swordsmen of VF-32

Tightly packed Tomcats!

anything else flying at the time. The Tomcat's distinctive weapon was the big Hughes 'AIM-54 Phoenix' AAM with a range of 125 miles and a fully active radar seeker, which allowed the missile to perform its terminal-phase attack on a target without requiring that the Tomcat keep it illuminated with radar. Operationally, the Tomcat could carry up to six Phoenix missiles, four in the fuselage tunnel between the engines and two on wing pylons, however in practice, a full armament load consisted usually of four Phoenix missiles on the tunnel stations, plus two AIM-9 Sparrow medium-range AAMs and two AIM-7 Sidewinder short-range AAMs.

The Phoenix and Sparrow were controlled by the powerful Hughes AN/AWG-9 radar and the AN/AWG-15 fire control computer. The AN/AWG-9 was inherited from the F-111B, and could search while tracking twenty-four targets, engage six targets simultaneously and look down into ground or sea clutter, detecting and tracking small targets flying at low level. Early F-14As were also fitted with a steerable AN/ALR-23 Infrared Search and Track (IRST) sensor under the nose that could be slaved to the radar or used independently. In the early 1980 however the IRST was replaced in Tomcat production with the Northrop AN/AXX-1 Television Camera Set (TCS), a steerable daylight video camera with a telephoto lens.

Under the original development plan, Grumman were to produce three versions: the F-14A as the standard aircraft with two Pratt &

Whitney TF30-P-412 engines; the F-14B with two P&W F401-PW-400, a derivative of the JTF-22 advanced powerplants; and the F-14C, essentially the F-14B with advanced avionics. The first operational unit received its F-14 in early 1973, but instead of 67 F-14As, the Navy received 556, the last delivered on 31 March 1987. There was no F-14B as originally defined, that designation being embraced by other variants. Instead the F-14A+ was the designation applied to the next Tomcat variant to be powered by the General Electric F110, but funding limits prevented the US Navy getting the more powerful version it wanted until the late 1980s. Initially, the F-14B designation was revived and given to the 'Super Tomcat' programme which pioneered the way for the F-14A+ and the F-14D, the latter being the definitive version with major avionics upgrades as well as more powerful engines.

The primary weakness of the F-14A was its TF-30 engines, which left the Tomcat distinctly underpowered and prone to frequent stagnation stalling. The Navy liked the Air Force's General Electric F110 and in February of 1984, announced that they would be adopting this engine for all future Tomcats. Thus in August 1984, the Navy awarded Grumman a contract for improved versions of the F-14. The new Tomcat would be known as the F-14D and the troublesome TF30 would be replaced by the F110-GE-400, the avionics would be upgraded from analogue to digital, the aircraft

Showing wings swept back this 'Pukin' Dogs F-14 from the USS George Washington speeds away

Grumman F-14A Tomcat 158991/NK of VF-1 'Wolfpack' aboard the USS Enterprise in 1976. Finished in Light Gull Gray FS16440 over White FS17875 and carries the high visibility markings that were the trademark of the US Navy in the 1970's

Grumman F-14D Tomcat, '103' of VF-31 'Tomcatters' aboard the USS John C Stennis circa 2005. The aircraft in finished in overall Light Ghost Gray FS36375, with Dark Ghost Gray FS36320 around the canopy and Gunship Gray FS36118 insignia and codes

Grumman F-14A Tomcat, 161276/NF of VF-154 'Black Knights' aboard the USS Kitty Hawk as part of Operation Iraqi Freedom circa early 2003. The aircraft is overall Light Ghost Gray FS36375, with Gunship Gray FS36118 insignia and codes with bright red unit tail markings

Grumman F-14 Tomcat, '13' of the NSAWC based at NAS Miramar in the late 1980's. This aircraft is painted in pseudo Iranian Air Force colours of Sand FS 30400, Dark Brown FS 30140 and Dark Green FS 34079 on the top and Light Ghost Gray FS 36622 on the underside. Later variations used IIRAF markings and national insignia

Grumman F-14D Tomcat 162926/AG of VF-143 'Pukin' Dogs' circa 2003. This aircraft is finished in overall Light Ghost Gray FS36375 with dark grey and black unit markings and full colour national insignia

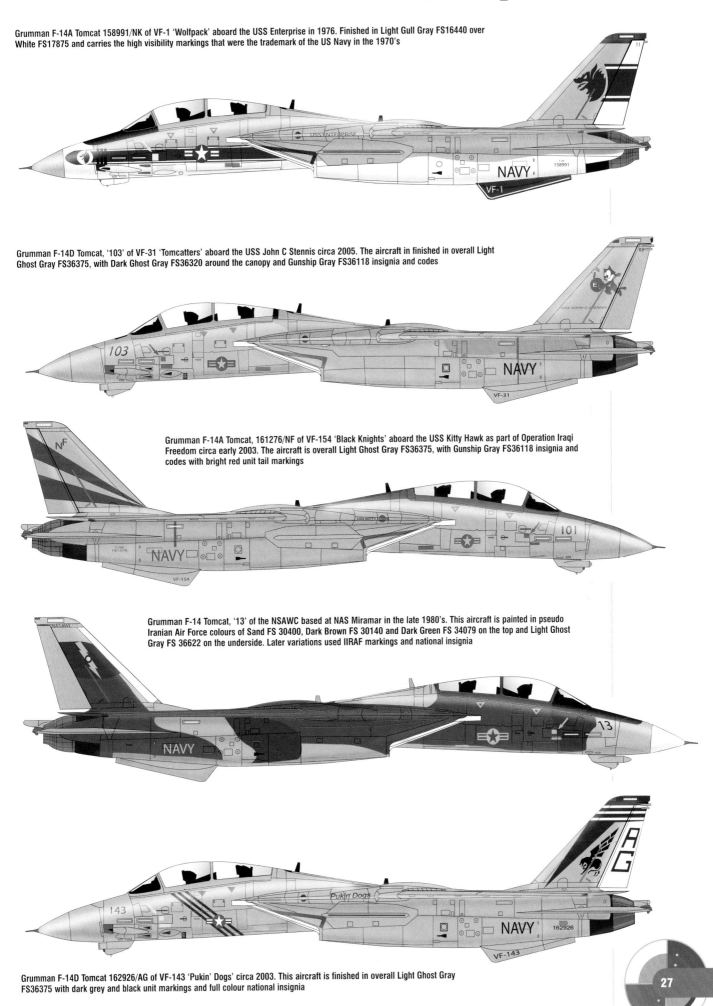

Loading up the internal 20mm cannon

would receive an enhanced radar, a new computer, a stores management system, new controls, new displays, and a digital INS. While the full F-14D avionics suite was being developed, an interim aircraft, designated F-14A+, would be produced and these aircraft would introduce the F110 engines but keep the F-14A electronics suite. However, it was planned that all F-14A+ aircraft would eventually be upgraded to full F-14D status. On May 1, 1991, the Navy decided to redesignate the F-14A+ as the F-14B, using the same designation as that of the stillborn F401-powered aircraft of 1973. A total of thirty-eight F-14Bs were newly built from scratch, and thirty-two additional F-14Bs produced by conversion from existing F-14A airframes.

The F-14D

Unlike the avionics of the F-14A which used largely analogue systems, the F-14D had a digital processing system based on MIL-STD-1553G multiprocessors linking the avionics units together and used the ASN-130 digital inertial navigational system, also of the F/A-18A. The new ASN-139 laser inertial navigation system was designed to be compatible with the -130 and the F-14D equipped with dual AYK-14 Standard Airborne Computers, and this gave the F-14D an improved detection and tracking range. The F-14D was also equipped with dual AYK-14 Standard Airborne Computers and its digital processors analyzed information from the radar, prioritize targets, and selected the weapons firing sequence. On the F-14A integration of the missiles was handled by the AWG-9, but on the F-14D this was undertaken by a digital stores management system. The avionics suite of the F-14D was centred on the Hughes AN/APG-71 radar which was a development of the APG-70 used in the F-15E Strike Eagle. The F-14D was provided with a dual chin pod under the nose that contained both a Northrop AN/AXX-1 Television Camera System (TCS) and a General Electric Infrared Search and Track (IRST) system. Previous Tomcat versions carried one or the other of these systems, but not both, and this system worked with the radar to identify the targets detected. The F-14D entered fleet service in July 1992 just too late for the Gulf War, and only fifty-five F-14D new-builds and conversions were produced which was just enough to equip three front-line squadrons - VF-2 'Bounty Hunters', VF-11 'Red

A Tomcat is directed onto the catapult track

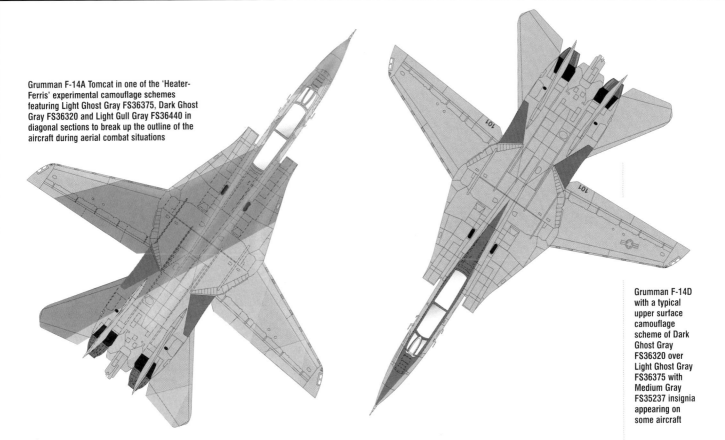

Grumman F-14A Tomcat in one of the 'Heater-Ferris' experimental camouflage schemes featuring Light Ghost Gray FS36375, Dark Ghost Gray FS36320 and Light Gull Gray FS36440 in diagonal sections to break up the outline of the aircraft during aerial combat situations

Grumman F-14D with a typical upper surface camouflage scheme of Dark Ghost Gray FS36320 over Light Ghost Gray FS36375 with Medium Gray FS35237 insignia appearing on some aircraft

Rippers', and VF-31 'Tomcatters'. In addition, part of the Pacific Fleet training unit VF-124 was equipped with F-14Ds.

Tomcat v Su-22

The first unit to become operational with the F-14D was VF-11 in July 1992. Perhaps the most famous Tomcat action took place when a pair of aircraft from VF-41 'Black Aces' downed a pair of Libyan Su-22s in the infamous 'Gulf of Sidra incident in August 1981. On the morning of the 19th, whilst undertaking an exercise outside the so-called 'Line OF Death' two VF-41 F-14As, call signs Fast Eagle 102, flown by Commander 'Hank' Kleeman and Lieutenant T 'DJ' Venlet and Fast Eagle 107 flown by Lieutenant 'Music' Muczynski and Lieutenant Junior Grade 'Amos' Anderson, were ordered to intercept and only few seconds before crossing, at an estimated distance of 300m, one of the two Libyans fired an AA-2 Atoll at one of the F-14s, which missed. Then the two Sukhois flew right past the Americans and tried to escape. The Tomcats evaded and were cleared to return fire in self defence on the hostile action. Kleeman went for the Fitter wingman while Muczynski went for the Su-22 leader. As the Su-22 turned clear of the sun Kleeman got a lock-on with an AIM-9L Sidewinder and fired, hitting the Su-22's tailpipe and the Libyan pilot was seen to eject successfully from his burning aircraft. Meanwhile, Muczynski fired on his lead Fitter at very close range with another AIM-9 destroying the Su-22.

Bombcat

For a while, an advanced bomb equipped F-14 Tomcat was regarded as an ideal replacement for the General Dynamics A-12 Avenger II, which was cancelled in December 1990. Initially, the Tomcat could carry only conventional dumb bombs, and had no precision-guided munition. It initially could not even carry or deliver laser-guided bombs and even after clearing the Tomcat for bomb carriage, the Navy still seemed half-hearted about the idea. However the idea of an

An F-14D Tomcat, assigned to the 'Tomcatters' of VF-31, deploys its fuel probe prior to aerial refueling during a mission over the Gulf'

Full afterburner night launches are always spectacular

29

attack Tomcat concept was building up momentum, driven in no short measure by the time gap between the phase-out of the A-6 Intruder and the arrival of the Super Hornet. Thereby the ability to deliver LGBs such as the GBU-10, GBU-12, GBU-16, and GBU-24 was added in 1994, although the Tomcat initially had to rely on other aircraft to designate the targets. The first GBU-16 bombs were dropped from a Tomcat of VF-103 on May 2, 1994 and Tomcats first dropped such bombs in anger on September 5, 1995 when two F-14s of VF-41 attacked targets in Serbia with GBU-16s, with F/A-18s painting the target with AN/AAS-38A Nite Hawk laser designators.

The Tomcat still lacked any type of dedicated FLIR and laser designator which would make it possible to operate at night and to deliver laser-guided bombs autonomously. Additionally the cost of a dedicated Tomcat system came far too expensive to be justified. The solution finally devised was a limited cheap and quick upgrade, with

Tomcats fire a volley of AIM-54 Phoenix missiles

A LANTIRN equipped F-14B takes on gas over Iraq

fit of the Martin-Marietta LANTIRN (Low Altitude Navigation and targeting Infra-Red for Night) pod which was selected to provide this capability. The LANTIRN Bombcat made its full combat debut during the Operation Desert Fox air strikes conducted against Iraq in December 1998, and the Bombcat saw more combat in the NATO air campaign against Serbia over Kosovo in the spring of 1999, flying hundreds of sorties.

Bye-Bye-Baby!

Sadly though, the Tomcat has now been added to the retirement list that already includes names such as the F-4 Phantom, A-6 Intruder, A-7 Corsair and A-4 Skyhawk, leaving a gap in the Carrier Battle

Groups that is going to be very hard to fill. The last American F-14s to fly a 'combat' mission, did so on the on 8 February 2006, when a pair of Tomcats landed aboard the USS Theodore Roosevelt after one dropped a bomb in Iraq. The 'bomber' aircraft was from VF-31 and the aircrew in question were pilot Lieutenant Justin Halligan and RIO Lieutenant Bill Frank. The other Tomcat on that mission was an F-14D from VF-213 piloted by Commander Air Wing Eight, Captain William G. Sizemore, and thus became the last F-14 pilot to land on an aircraft carrier after a 'combat' mission. The USS Theodore Roosevelt shot an F-14D assigned to VF-31 from its catapult for the last time on 28 July 2006, piloted by Lieutenant Blake Coleman & RIO Lieutenant Commander Dave Lauderbaugh. The last ever trap recovery was made by Lieutenant Chris Rattigan & Lieutenant Paul Dort.

Losing the Tomcat has meant losing the abilities of two excellent aircraft, the fighting capabilities of the F-14, and the all-weather bombing ability of the A-6E Intruder, which the F-14D did in some way pick up the slack from. With the loss of the Grumman Tomcat, there is no longer a Grumman fighter on America's carrier decks, something that has not happened since the 1930s! The legend of the 'Grumman Iron Works' carried on by the Wildcat, Hellcat, Tigercat, Bearcat, Panther, Cougar, and Tiger has now ended with the Tomcat. ⬛

One of the 'Tomcatters' F-14Ds prepares to 'ride the cat' Note the depression of the nosewheel in preparation for flinging the aircraft off the deck

After the September 11 attacks, no less then eight F-14 squadrons participated in Operation Enduring Freedom

A 'Black Lions' F-14D in concert with an S-3 Viking. Note the low-visibility tactical paint scheme

F-14A 158627 being rolled out – what a superb sight!

Jump Jets
The AV-8B Harrier II
Versatile VSTOL strike platform

The operational success of the AV-8A/C confirmed the US Marine Corps belief in VSTOL technology and its advantages their particular type of warfare. What was needed now was a follow-on aircraft that met their future requirements for a 'light attack' aircraft that carried a 'big punch'. Their search gathered together studies undertaken by McDonnell Douglas, following their aborted AV-16 effort, and led to the collaborative 'AV-8B Advanced Harrier Program' with British Aerospace.

Central to this new breed of Harrier was an advanced 'big-wing', originally proposed by Hawker and derived from NASA based technology of supercritical aerofoils. Also to achieve the maximum benefits in terms of weight saving, advanced structural materials were used instead of traditional metal, and a unique graphite epoxy construction gave the AV-8B the first carbon-fibre technology wing fitted to a military aircraft. At the rear of the wing a large, single-slotted

flap was integrated to support the jet efflux from the engine nozzles, which increased take-off lift and helped to arrest the loss of performance during vertical landings. The outrigger wheels were also moved inboard to better facilitate rough field work, and the `elephant's ear' engine intakes were also redesigned and increased in size, initially with a double row of suction relief doors (later revised to a single row) and the forward cold-air nozzles reshaped to a `zero-scarf' design. These two features alone added an amazing 800lb of thrust.

In late 1976, as part of the original 'Phase I' of the 'Advanced Harrier Program' two Harrier Technology Demonstrators, both remanufactured AV-8As (158394 and 158395) as well as a full-scale wind tunnel test vehicle (158385) were produced. YAV-8B No.1, 158394 flew on 9 November 1978, and the second, YAV-813, 158395, flew on 19 February 1979. The engine carried was the Pegasus II F402-RR-404 with 21,700lb of thrust, and included a new gearbox

The nose profile of the Harrier II Plus with its radome and FLIR housing. Note also the 100% LERX and the enlarged fire access inlets.

and zero-scarf forward nozzles and the same LID improvements as were added to the AV-8C. Following on from the two YAV-8Bs came 161396 the first of four FSD (Full Scale Development) aircraft, after which came an initial batch of twelve production AV-8Bs, and a limited run of a further twenty-one aircraft. FSD Harrier 161396 made its first tentative hover flight on 5 November 1981. Under a work-share agreement, British Aerospace were responsible for the centre and rear fuselage sections, the fin and rudder, the centreline pylon and the reaction control system, and Rolls-Royce had the role of supplying the Pegasus engine, the remainder being supplied by McDonnell Douglas who also undertook assembly. The ejector seat fitted was the UPC/Stencel 10B, with zero-zero capabilities.

The avionics themselves were in the main new brand new although some were unashamedly borrowed from other McDonnell Douglas programmes. In the nose was a Hughes ARBS (Angle-Rate Bombing System), with a TV and dual mode tracker facility, projecting its information on to a Smiths Industries upgraded SU-128/A HUD or the pilots MFD (Multi-Function Display) onto which could be shown sensor information, nav/mission plots, ARN/118 TACAN information, engine data and SAAHS (Stability Augmentation and Attitude Hold System) updates. Some of the

cockpit interfaces were borrowed from the F-18 - items such as the improved HOTAS (hands-on-throttle and-stick) controls, the AYK-14 mission computer, the ASN-130 INS, the Lear Siegler AN/AYQ-13 stores management system, and the ECM-resistant fibre optic cables. The RWR and underfuselage AN/ALE-39 chaff and flare dispensers were the same as those used on the AV-8C programme and all aircraft information was fed through a 1553A databus. Communications were provided by two ARC-182 wide band UHF/VHF radios, and the ECM suite included the highly efficient AN/ALR-67 RWR system. To add more muscle to its attack potential a new gun, the General Electric GAU-12A Equaliser was developed, the gun itself being housed in the left-hand pod, with 300 rounds of ammunition in the right-hand pod.

The four FSDs, the twelve 'initial production' and the twenty-one 'limited production' aircraft were fitted with an interim F402-RR-404A engine, however the production batch proper were fitted with

When embarked on assault ships a Harrier detachment will invariable wear the codes of the lead squadron attached to that ship. Hence this pair of Harriers from VMA-513 carry the codes of HMM-163 aboard USS Boxer.

The Night Attack Harrier carries a FLIR atop the nose section as modelled here by 164128 of VMA-211

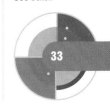

33

the definitive F404-RR-406, with zero-scarf front nozzles and the DECS (Digital Engine Control System) controls. The first aircraft that would bear the name 'Harrier II' was officially rolled out on 16 October 1981 and was used to undertake initial hovering trials. This aircraft was not fitted with the LERX (Leading Edge Root Extensions) and still carried the YAV-B style double-row intake doors. VMAT-203 received its first AV-8B in a ceremony on 12 January 1984, when it was officially handed 161573/KD-21. VMA-331, 'The Bumblebees' was the first of the front-line 'gun squadrons' to get its hands on the AV-8B, and this was followed at Cherry Point by VMA-231, VMA-223 and VMA-542, while at Yuma VMA-513 (which stood down the Marines' last AV-8C in August 1986 for the AV-8B). VMA-211 and VMA311 also traded-up for the Harrier II and thus far only one Harrier unit has been stood down in consequence of the post-Cold War cutbacks: the AV-8Bs of VMA-331 were decommissioned in October 1992.

'Night Attack'

The ability to operate their Harriers 'after dark' was of great importance to the US Marine Corps philosophy and a 'proof of concept' aircraft, AV-8B 162966, complete with night-attack suite, was produced and fitted with a GEC Sensors FLIR, mounted in front of the cockpit, atop the nose section and above and to the rear of the Hughes AN/ASB-19 Angle Rate Bombing System (ARBS), and within near direct line of sight for the pilot. Trials were then undertaken using the first production aircraft 163853 beginning 8 July 1989 and the fist 'Night Attack' Harrier proper was delivered into squadron service on 15 September of that year. Originally the aircraft type was to be the AV-8D - however AV-8B(NA) was universally accepted at its designation. Also included on the airframe were upward and downward firing AN/ALE-39 chaff and flare dispensers with the upward firing ones being scabbed onto the topside of the rear fuselage. These aircraft were also fitted (and some retro-fitted) with the 100% LERX fairing at the wing roots and the F402-RR408-11-61 engine. The first unit to take on charge the new breed was VMA-214,

A Night Attack Harrier amongst its II Plus cousins.

'The Black Sheep' on 1 September 1989 at MCAS Yuma, followed by VMA-211 'The Wake Island Avengers'. These were followed by VMA311 'The Tomcats', which traded up its 'vanilla' AV-8Bs in May 1992, and VMA-513, 'The Flying Nightmares', which also traded up in September 1992. VMA-233 was the only Cherry Point unit to use the night attack model from 1992, until converting to the Harrier II Plus in June 1994.

A pair of Harriers prepare to take on fuel

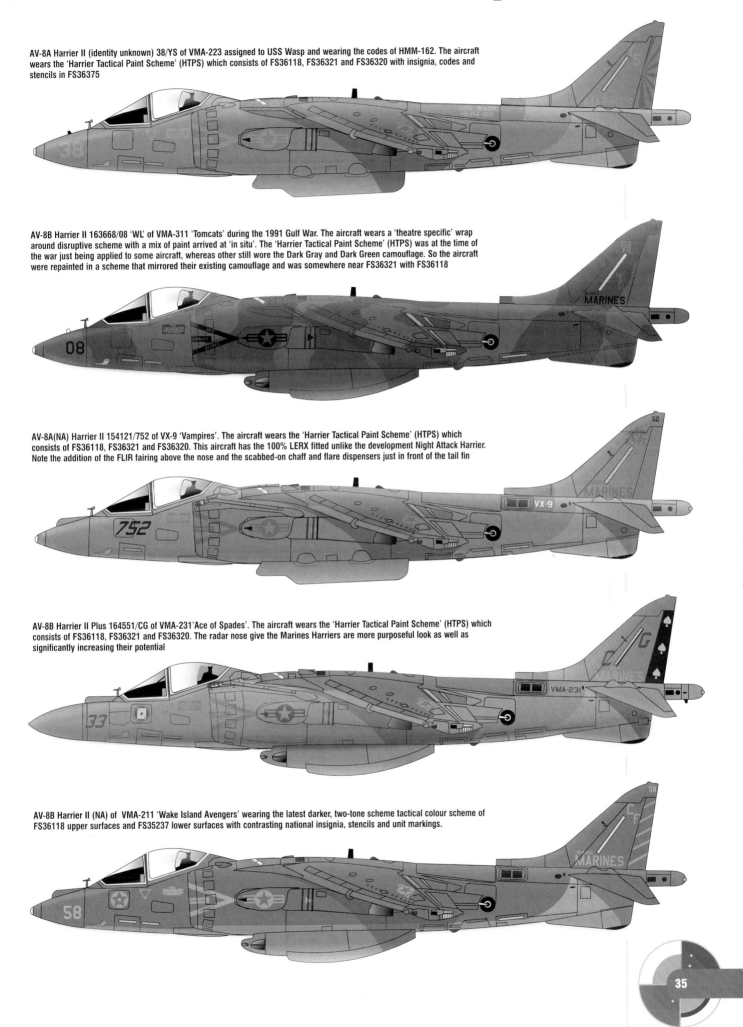

AV-8A Harrier II (identity unknown) 38/YS of VMA-223 assigned to USS Wasp and wearing the codes of HMM-162. The aircraft wears the 'Harrier Tactical Paint Scheme' (HTPS) which consists of FS36118, FS36321 and FS36320 with insignia, codes and stencils in FS36375

AV-8B Harrier II 163668/08 'WL' of VMA-311 'Tomcats' during the 1991 Gulf War. The aircraft wears a 'theatre specific' wrap around disruptive scheme with a mix of paint arrived at 'in situ'. The 'Harrier Tactical Paint Scheme' (HTPS) was at the time of the war just being applied to some aircraft, whereas other still wore the Dark Gray and Dark Green camouflage. So the aircraft were repainted in a scheme that mirrored their existing camouflage and was somewhere near FS36321 with FS36118

AV-8A(NA) Harrier II 154121/752 of VX-9 'Vampires'. The aircraft wears the 'Harrier Tactical Paint Scheme' (HTPS) which consists of FS36118, FS36321 and FS36320. This aircraft has the 100% LERX fitted unlike the development Night Attack Harrier. Note the addition of the FLIR fairing above the nose and the scabbed-on chaff and flare dispensers just in front of the tail fin

AV-8B Harrier II Plus 164551/CG of VMA-231'Ace of Spades'. The aircraft wears the 'Harrier Tactical Paint Scheme' (HTPS) which consists of FS36118, FS36321 and FS36320. The radar nose give the Marines Harriers are more purposeful look as well as significantly increasing their potential

AV-8B Harrier II (NA) of VMA-211 'Wake Island Avengers' wearing the latest darker, two-tone scheme tactical colour scheme of FS36118 upper surfaces and FS35237 lower surfaces with contrasting national insignia, stencils and unit markings.

'Radar Raiders'

The original concept of a radar-equipped Harrier was first mooted in a 1988 Marine Corps requirement for an upgraded AV-8 that could carry out attacks by both day and night, without regard for weather conditions. McDonnell Douglas was thus awarded a contract on 3 December 1990 for the radar equipped 'Harrier II Plus', and aircraft 164129, fitted with an APG-65Q4 radar of F/A-18 Hornet fame took to the air on 22 September 1992. The Harrier II Plus retains all the avionics and airframe changes of the successful Night Attack Harrier, including the FLIR and upward and downward firing chaff/flare launchers and the powerful Rolls-Royce Pegasus F402-RR408 engine, the installation of the 100% LERX, GPS receiver and provision for the AIM-120 AMRAAM missile. Also included was a Missile Approach Warning System (MAWS), the external 'eye' of which can be found in a faceted sensor beneath the aircraft's nose. This sensor detects `flashes' and missile plumes by scanning in the ultraviolet and providing both a visual and an audible warning in the cockpit. The first deliveries to squadron service began in June 1993, and a Marines programme then called for all the 'vanilla' AV-8Bs to be converted to II Plus in a concerted effort to standardise the Harrier fleet, and for twenty-seven new airframes to be produced. In reality only seventy-three rebuilds were authorised.

A brace of AV-8B(NA) Night Attack birds wearing the HTPS (Harrier Tactical Paint Scheme) colours and hailing from VMA-211 'Wake Island Avengers'

'War Wagons'

The US Marines Harriers first went to war during Operation Desert Storm where they operated from King Abdul Aziz Air Base (KAAAB), and a FARP (Forward Area Rearm/Refuel Point) at a helicopter base at Tanajib. Aircraft from VMA-311, VMA-542 and VMA-231 all took part in the conflict, and the Harriers wore a 'theatre specific' disruptive paint scheme of a light and dark grey disruptive wrap around nature, mirroring their traditional grey and green scheme. These 'in the field' hues were created by taking the basic Marine Corps grey and adding 'coffee cups' of black until the desired shade was achieved! Further war roles followed in Bosnia and Somalia, and more recently in a return to the Gulf in Operation Iraqi Freedom, and latterly Operation 'Enduring Freedom' in Afghanistan. New weaponry has also been added in the shape of JDAM (Joint Direct Attack Munitions) and precision guided bombs, and to facilitate the delivery of such weapons the Marine Corps has purchased the Rafael 'Litening' pod, a 'class-act' according to Harrier pilots.

VSTOL will remain a vital part of the Marines philosophy and will continue with the arrival of the F-35B. However, the Harrier will always have a special place in the annals of Marine Corps aviation. **CS**

Wearing the new darker grey camouflage a very clean AV-8B (NA) Harrier of VMA-211 'Wake Island Avengers' as it comes aboard the USS Essex

Two-pair! A couple of Night Attack Harriers intermingled with a brace of radar equipped II Plus birds.

Long Range Kill

The AIM-54 Phoenix

Teeth of the Tomcat

The Hughes AIM-54A Phoenix missile was the primary armament of the F-14, and the Tomcat was originally designed with this missile in mind. The Phoenix missile was propelled by a single-stage Rocketdyne MK47 solid-fuel rocket motor, which gave it a velocity at burnout of Mach 3.8 at low altitudes, although Mach 5 could be achieved at high altitudes in the long-range mode. The missile had four fixed delta-shaped wings and was steered by tail-mounted control surfaces. On trials, the missile was seen to be able to manoeuvre at 17 g. The fuselage and aerodynamic surfaces of the Phoenix were made from metal, but the fuselage was covered with ablative thermal insulation. Dimensionally the missile was 13.2 feet long, the body 13 inches wide, the wing span 3 feet and the launch weight about 985 pounds. The missile had a 132 pound annular blast fragmentation high-explosive warhead.

After launch, the Phoenix could use three different types of guidance - autopilot, semi-active radar homing, and fully-active radar homing. For long-range shots, the missile generally flew a pre-programmed route immediately after launch under autopilot control. At midcourse, the nose-mounted radar seeker took over, operating in semi-active mode, homing in on radar waves reflected off the target from the Tomcat's AWG-9 radar. Once within about 14 miles of the

target, the Phoenix's own DSQ-26 radar took over for the final run in to the target, and the missile operated in fully-active radar homing mode. At this time the missile was completely independent of its launching aircraft, and became truly 'fire-and-forget'.

One of the more advanced features of the AWG-9/Phoenix weapons system was the ability to track and engage multiple targets at the same time. Track-While-Scan (TWS) mode would be used for multiple-target tracking and multi-shot Phoenix engagements. In TWS mode, the AWG-9 could carry out simultaneous long-range missile attacks against up to six targets, while tracking 24 more. As each target within the region of sky being scanned was detected, the AWG-9 determined its range and angular position and this information was passed along to the computer where it was compared to the predicted positions of the targets already detected. If the newly-detected target could be correlated with an already-known target, the target's track file would be updated with its current position. If not, then a new track file was opened for what was presumed to be a new target. The computer then assigned threat priorities to each track. In this mode, each target was not continually illuminated by the radar, and the Phoenix missile guidance system received only samples of radar data. Maximum missile range in this

Note here the portable jacking system to load the heavy missile

mode was about 90 km.

In Range-While-Search (RWS) mode, the set provided range and angular data without stopping the normal antenna TWS search pattern. In Pulse-Doppler Single-Target Track (PDSTT) mode, when a single target is to be tracked, the AWG-9 antenna would be locked on to a single long-range target at ranges of up to 130 km. The missile could then be launched at 100 km range. A Jam Angle Track (JAT) facility could be use to provide range, speed, and angular information on targets being protected by ECM. In this mode, the radar could also be slaved to the aircraft's electro-optical sighting unit. The AWG-9 also had conventional pulse modes for use at short and medium ranges.

On maximum-range missions, the Phoenix was usually lofted into a high trajectory designed to reduce interference between the AWG-9's powerful transmitter and the missile's receiving system. The flight time on such missions could be up to three minutes. The Tomcat had the capability of carrying up to six Phoenix missiles, four on individual pallets mounted underneath the fuselage and one on each of the fixed wing glove pylons and the missile was designed for ejection launch using the LAU-93 or LAU-132 launchers. However, in typical operations, the usual weapons load would be four Phoenix, two Sparrows, and two Sidewinders. The original specification called for six Phoenix missiles, but it was found that the deck impacts during carrier landings were too hard when carrying that many missiles, so a full load of six was rarely, if ever carried.

The AIM-54A was approved for service use on January 28, 1975. The AIM-54B had improved resistance to jamming, and was introduced into service in 1983. It had sheet-metal wings and fins instead of honeycomb structure, non-liquid hydraulic and thermal conditioning system, and somewhat simplified engineering.

The later AIM-54C had a higher-thrust motor, an improved warhead, fully solid-state electronics, and an improved fuse that was better capable of detonating the warhead at the precise moment to maximize its destructive effect on the target. The AIM-54C also had better electronic counter-countermeasures capability, allowing it to cope with small, low-altitude targets, being able to discriminate between the true target and any 'chaff' that might be released in an attempt to break lock-on.

On 5 January 1999 a pair of F-14Ds on patrol over Iraq encountered two Iraqi MiG-25s. The Tomcats fired two AIM-54 Phoenix missiles (one each), the first ever combat Phoenix launch by the US Navy, however the Iraqi jets turned back north and the missiles failed to hit their targets. When production ceased in the early 1990s, more than 5,000 AIM-54 missiles of all versions had been built, about half of these being AIM-54Cs. By the early 2000s, all operational missiles were of the AIM-54C variant, the remaining AIM-54As having been placed in storage and with the impending retirement of the Tomcat, the Navy officially retired the AIM-54 from fleet service on 30 September 2004. ▣

A rarely seen sight – for publicity purposes only – six Phoenix missiles on one Tomcat!

An AIM-54C is wheeled out for fitting to an F-14. Note the protective nose cover

An AIM-54C uploaded and ready to go

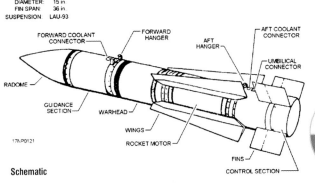

WEIGHT: 1000 lb
DIMENSIONS:
  LENGTH: 156 in.
  DIAMETER: 15 in.
  FIN SPAN: 36 in.
SUSPENSION: LAU-93

FORWARD COOLANT CONNECTOR
FORWARD HANGER
AFT HANGER
AFT COOLANT CONNECTOR
UMBILICAL CONNECTOR
RADOME
GUIDANCE SECTION
WARHEAD
WINGS
ROCKET MOTOR
FINS
CONTROL SECTION

17NP0121

Schematic

Glide Bomb

AGM-154 JSOW

Joint Stand-Off Weapon

A JSOW ready to be 'hung' aboard a host aircraft

The AGM-154 JSOW is a family of low cost, highly lethal glide weapons that is revolutionising aerial strike warfare. The AGM-154 JSOW uses flip-out wings and four cruciform (plus two small horizontal) tailfins for flight control. The glide range of the weapon is some is 28km (15nm) for low-altitude and up to 74km (40nm) for high-altitude launches. This new generation of glide weapon ensures the host aircraft has a higher survivability rate by enabling precision air strikes from well beyond the range of most enemy air defences. JSOW variants are guided to their targets by a highly integrated Global Positioning System and Inertial Measurement System (GPS/IMS), and each JSOW can receive targeting information in a totally 'pre-briefed' mode or via 'targeting updates' received whilst airborne through onboard sensors or from other suitably equipped aircraft. With its modular design JSOW's variants integrate different lethal sub-munitions as well as blast/fragmentation and penetrating warheads making it ideal for

soft area targets, armoured vehicles and hardened targets. JSOW, which integrates the BLU-97, Combined Effects Bomblets and the BLU-108 Sensor Fused Weapon sub-munitions has been in operation since 1999, debuting in Operation Southern Watch, and playing a pivotal role in Operations Allied Force, Enduring Freedom and Iraqi Freedom and currently in Afghanistan.

JSOW is currently available in three variants: The AGM-154A variant uses a cluster bomb dispenser with 145 BLU-97/B CEM (Combined Effects Munition) bomblets (1.54 kg (3.4 lb) each) for use against soft targets. The AGM-154B carries 6 BLU-108/B SFM (Sensor Fused Munition) dispensers, each of which can release four 'Skeet' terminally guided anti-tank sub-munitions, and the AGM-154C (developed for the Navy only) uses a 'BROACH' multi-stage penetrator warhead, developed by BAE Systems. It also features an IIR seeker and ATA (Autonomous Target Acquisition) technology (similar to that of the AGM-84K SLAM-ER). JSOW is currently flying on the F/A-18, F-15E, F-16, B-52, B-1 and B-2 and is also an option for the F-35 JSF.

Those traffic cones get everywhere! This one is unlucky though!

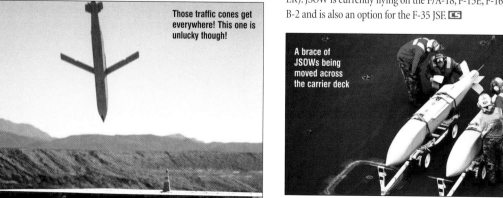

A brace of JSOWs being moved across the carrier deck

SLAMMER
AGM-84K SLAM-ER
'Standoff Land Attack Missile-Expanded Response'

The US Navy's AGM-84K Standoff Land Attack Missile-Expanded Response SLAM-ER, is an evolutionary upgrade to the combat-proven SLAM, an air-launched, day/night, adverse weather, over-the-horizon, precision strike missile. SLAM-ER features a highly accurate, GPS-aided guidance system; an imaging infrared seeker and two-way data-link with the AWW-13 Advanced Data Link pod; improved missile aerodynamic performance that allows both long and short range and attack profiles. SLAM-ER is the first weapon to feature Automatic Target Acquisition that helps improve target acquisition in cluttered scenes and overcomes most IR countermeasures. The SLAM-ER can be launched and controlled by F/A-18C/D/E/F, P-3 Orions, and S-3 Viking platforms and its roots go back to the original Harpoon anti-ship missile placed in fleet service in the late 1970s, and because of emerging operational requirements, the Standoff Land Attack Missile (SLAM) was devised as a derivative. This baseline SLAM missile system was developed and fielded in less than 48 months, and was successfully employed by F/A-18 and A-6 aircrews in 'Desert Storm' even before operational testing had begun! SLAM-ER has been used in all operational theatres since and provides the US Navy with a valuable stand-off capability. **CS**

A head-on view of a SLAM-ER being loaded aboard an F/A-18

A SLAM-ER being fitted to a P-3 Orion

The data-link pod for the SLAM-ER

War Hoover
The Lockheed S-3 Viking
Sub-hunter and beyond

A very colourful pair from VS-21

The Viking was originally conceived for use by the US Navy to hunt and destroy enemy submarines and provide surveillance of surface shipping. This compact, subsonic, all-weather, multi-mission aircraft has a commendably long range, and carries an automated weapon systems and is capable of even longer missions with in-flight refuelling. Because of the engines' high-pitched sound, it carries the nickname of the 'Hoover' after the popular brand of vacuum cleaner.

The S-3 was designed by Lockheed with assistance from Ling-Temco-Vought and UNIVAC to fit the United States Navy VSX (Heavier-than-air, Anti-submarine, Experimental) requirement as a replacement for the piston-engined Grumman S-2 Tracker. Since Lockheed had no experience in building carrier-based aircraft, LTV

17 Ready for the fastest fairground ride in the world!

was responsible for construction of the folding wings and tail, the engine nacelles, and the landing gear which was derived from the A-7 Corsair II (nose) and the F-8 Crusader (main). UNIVAC built the onboard computers which integrated input from sensors and sonobuoys. The first prototype flew on 1 January 1972 and entered service in 1974. During its four-year production run some 186 S-3As were built.

The S-3 has a conventional monoplane structure with a high-mounted cantilever wing, swept back 15°, and is powered by two turbofan engines mounted in nacelles under the wings. The aircraft can seat four crew members with the pilot and the co-pilot/tactical coordinator (COTAC) in the front of the cockpit and the tactical coordinator (TACCO) and sensor operator (SENSO) in the back. All crew members sit on upward-firing zero-zero ejector seats. The wing is fitted with leading edge and Fowler flaps, and spoilers are fitted to both the upper and the lower surfaces of the wings. The aircraft also has two underwing hardpoints that can be used to carry fuel tanks, general purpose and cluster bombs, missiles, rockets, and storage pods. It also has four internal bomb bay sections that can also be used to carry GP bombs and torpedos. A number of sonobuoy chutes are also fitted, and there are three dispensers for chaff and flares, and for their anti-submarine role a retractable magnetic anomaly detector (MAD) boom is fitted in the tail.

The S-3A officially became operational with the VS-41 Shamrocks Fleet Replacement Squadron. The first operational cruise took place in July 1978 with VS-21 'Fighting Redtails' aboard USS John F. Kennedy (CV-67). During 1991, some of the Vikings were upgraded to S-3B standard with a number of new sensors, avionics, and weapons systems, including the capability tof launching the AGM-84 Harpoon anti-ship missile. The S-3B can also be fitted with 'buddy-buddy refuelling pod to allow the Viking to refuel other aircraft. Sixteen S-3As were further converted to ES-3 Shadows for carrier-based electronic reconnaissance (ELINT) duties and a few aircraft, designated US-3A, were also converted for utility and limited cargo duty. Plans were also made to develop a dedicated KS-3A carrier-based tanker aircraft to replace the retired KA-6 but these were ultimately cancelled.

Since the submarine threat for which the Viking was conceived has substantially diminished, the 'Hoovers' have had the majority of their ASW kit removed and are now used primarily for Sea Control duties such as surface search, sea and ground attack, over-the-horizon targeting, and aerial refuelling. As a result, crews are now usually limited to two, though three-person crews are not unusual with certain missions.

A number of more recent upgrade programs have been implemented. These include the Carrier Airborne Inertial Navigation System II (CAINS II) system, an additional GPS has been fitted, as well as new electronic flight instruments (EFI). The Maverick Plus System (MPS) has added the capability to employ the AGM-65E laser-guided or AGM-65F IR missile, and the latest SLAM/ER cruise missile is also in the aircraft arsenal with its associated AWW-13 data link pod.

The S-3B saw extensive service during the 1991 Gulf War, performing attack, tanker, and ELINT duties, and launching copious numbers of ADM-114 TALD Decoys. Navy's 'Sundown Plan' for its Vikings calls for the gradual disestablishment of operational units as the number of F/A-18E/F squadrons increase. The F/A-18 will eventually take over the aerial tanking role from the S-3, thus when an air wing receives its first Super Hornet squadron, its Viking squadron reduces its number of jets from eight to six. When that air wing receives its second Super Hornet squadron, the Viking squadron disestablishes. But that's not the end of the story, as VS-32 the Maulers, aboard the USS Enterprise in late 2006 were given a new piece of kit in the shape of the AN/AAQ-14 LANTRIN pod used for surface surveillance and deep reconnaissance tasks inside Iraq, So even with its impending retirement, the 'Hoover' is still being given new tasks, quire a testament to the aircraft's versatility!

On May 1, 2003, US President George W. Bush rode in the co-pilot seat of a Viking that landed on the USS Abraham Lincoln, where he delivered his 'Mission Accomplished' speech announcing the end of major combat in the 2003 invasion of Iraq. This was the only Navy flight to date to use the call sign 'Navy One'. **CS**

Close-in on the IFR probe and canopy detailing

In addition to their folding wings the Vikings also have folding tails!

A brace of Vidars from VS-22 display their refuelling prowess!

A colourful Viking of Sea Control Squadron 41 'The Shamrocks'

Viking Variants

- S-3A First production version, 186 built.

- S-3B Upgraded avionics, AN/APS-137 inverse synthetic aperture radar, Joint Tactical Information Distribution System, AGM-84 Harpoon launch capability, first flight 1984-09-13, 119 converted from S-3As.

- ES-3 Shadow ELINT aircraft, AN/APS-137 inverse synthetic aperture radar, first flight 1991-05-15, 16 converted from S-3A.

- KS-3A Proposed dedicated air tanker with fuel capacity of 4,382 US gal (16,600 L), one converted from YS-3A, later converted to US-3A.

- KS-3B Proposed air tanker based on S-3B and utilizing the buddy refuelling system, not built.

- US-3A S-3A modified for carrier onboard delivery, capacity for six passengers or 4,680 lb (2,120 kg) of cargo, retired in 1998.

- Alladin Viking Classified modifications, used in the Bosnian War

- Beartrap Viking S-3Bs fitted with still-classified modifications.

- Callypso Viking Proposed anti-smuggling variant, not built.

- Gray Wolf Viking One aircraft fitted with AN/APG-76 radar in a modified cargo pod under the wing. Also dubbed SeaSTARS in reference to E-8 Joint STARS.

- Orca Viking Avionics testbed.

- Outlaw Viking One S-3B fitted with Over-the-horizon Airborne Sensor Information System (OASIS III), returned to regular S-3B in 1998.

A busy deck scene as an S-3 prepares to ride the 'cat'

Great view of the underside bays and sonobuoy hatches

Shadow Vikings

The ES-3A

Sophisticated ELINT platform

On 21 January 1972, the first flight of the Navy's S-3A Viking ushered in a new era in under sea warfare. Built by Lockheed, the carrier based, twin-turbofan jet dramatically improved the anti-submarine and surface surveillance capability of the Navy. With the passing of the venerable EA-3B Skywarrior, or 'Whale' in Navy parlance during the early 1990's, the service lost a considerable ELINT capability and the Navy looked at their existing stock of aircraft in order to find a suitable replacement. This was found in the S-3 Viking. In all some sixteen S-3 airframes were modified to the new ES-3 standard, and to accommodate this new role the S-3's anti-submarine gear was removed and the bomb-bay converted to avionics racks to house new sensors. In addition a spine fairing with bulbous sensor pack was added, and the aircraft sprouted a plethora of antennae commensurate with its new role.

A brace of VQ-6 birds 'hook down' for a carrier approach

An ES-3A of VQ-6 'The Ravens' aboard the USS George Washington. Note the avionics fairing on the spine

The ES-3As mounted very sophisticated systems, including full-spectrum RF receivers, DF equipment, a variety of recording and measuring sensors, GPS navigation systems, a complete communications suite with avionics based on the Aries II system of the land-based EP-3E Orion. They also retained the S-3's inverse synthetic aperture radar, FLIR, and ESM equipment, and carried a crew of four comprising of a pilot, an NFO, and two Systems Operators. Advanced sensor, navigation and communications systems allowed the crew to collect extensive data, and distribute that high-quality information through a variety of channels to the carrier battle group. This gave the battle group commander a clear picture of potential airborne, surface and sub-surface threats.

Systems enhancements and upgrades to the electronic support systems were introduced to the ES-3 once test and evaluation has been completed by VX-1 and in 1998 the ES-3A completed delivery of Fleet Issue 4 and common improvement program, which added

the AN/ARC-187 radio and replaced the AN/USH-26 recorders and the ES-3A also completed a system design review for the Joint Airborne Signal Intelligence Compliance Program. Powered by two TF34-GE-2 engines, the sixteen aircraft were split between two squadrons, VQ-5 'Sea Shadows' in the Pacific Fleet and VQ-6 'Ravens' in the Atlantic Fleet. Detachments of two or three aircraft were normally deployed with every carrier air group, providing ESM, SIGINT and OTH support.

The first ES-3A was delivered in 1991, and the last in 1993 and the Shadow had been deployed with every CVBG. However, in 1998 the US Navy realised that it could not afford to fund the upgrades necessary need to keep the aircraft viable through to 2013. So the two squadrons began retiring their aircraft to AMARC at Davis Monthan AFB Arizona in Jan 1999 and by May 1999 all the aircraft had been withdrawn from service with the last two-plane detachment deploying aboard the USS Enterprise. **CS**

The ES-3 retained all of the shipboard abilities of the Viking

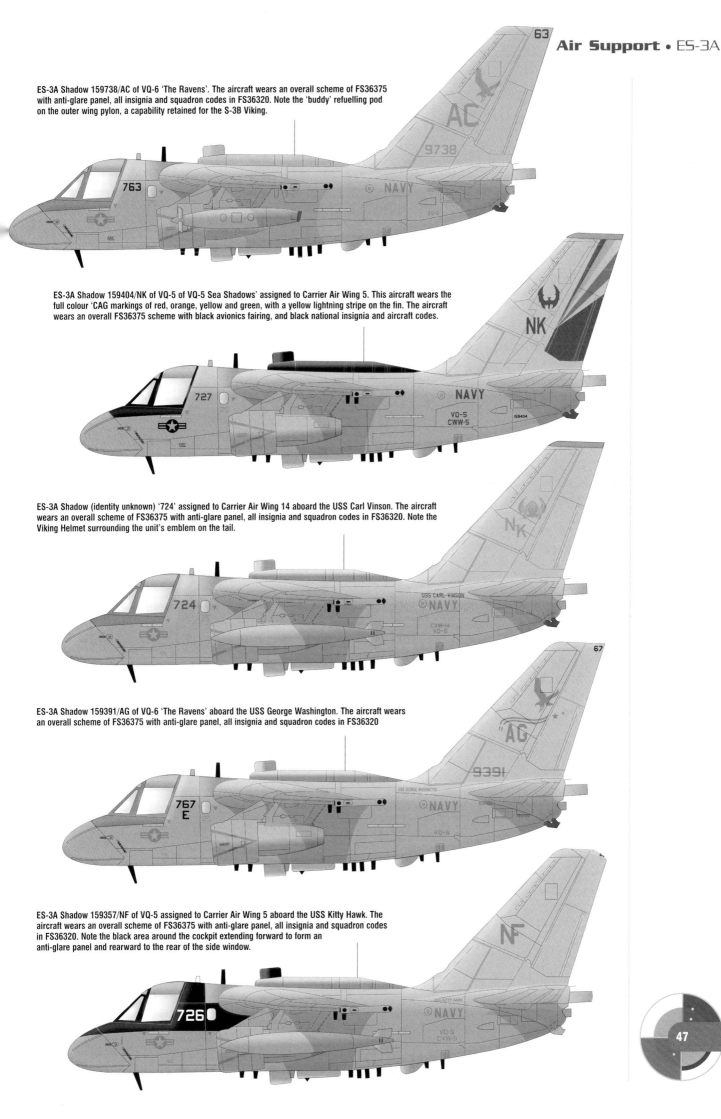

ES-3A Shadow 159738/AC of VQ-6 'The Ravens'. The aircraft wears an overall scheme of FS36375 with anti-glare panel, all insignia and squadron codes in FS36320. Note the 'buddy' refuelling pod on the outer wing pylon, a capability retained for the S-3B Viking.

ES-3A Shadow 159404/NK of VQ-5 of VQ-5 Sea Shadows' assigned to Carrier Air Wing 5. This aircraft wears the full colour 'CAG markings of red, orange, yellow and green, with a yellow lightning stripe on the fin. The aircraft wears an overall FS36375 scheme with black avionics fairing, and black national insignia and aircraft codes.

ES-3A Shadow (identity unknown) '724' assigned to Carrier Air Wing 14 aboard the USS Carl Vinson. The aircraft wears an overall scheme of FS36375 with anti-glare panel, all insignia and squadron codes in FS36320. Note the Viking Helmet surrounding the unit's emblem on the tail.

ES-3A Shadow 159391/AG of VQ-6 'The Ravens' aboard the USS George Washington. The aircraft wears an overall scheme of FS36375 with anti-glare panel, all insignia and squadron codes in FS36320

ES-3A Shadow 159357/NF of VQ-5 assigned to Carrier Air Wing 5 aboard the USS Kitty Hawk. The aircraft wears an overall scheme of FS36375 with anti-glare panel, all insignia and squadron codes in FS36320. Note the black area around the cockpit extending forward to form an anti-glare panel and rearward to the rear of the side window.

Electronic Intruders

The EA-6A

Combat Countermeasures

EA-6A 156981/AA of VAQ-309. Note the chaff and flare pod on the outer pylon

The EA-6A was an Electronic Warfare/ECM version of the A-6 Intruder which was developed early in the aircraft's life specifically for use by the US Marine Corps, which needed a new ECM platform to replace its elderly F3D-2Q Skynights. Initially designated the A2F-1Q, a derivative of the A2F-1, the Marines' interest was such that they ordered the aircraft in the March of 1962, after which it was redesignated as the EA-6A in September of that year.

EA-6A 156988/GD of VAQ-33. The most significant external change was the presence of a canoe-shaped fin-tip fairing

Two A2F-1s were modified as prototypes for the A2F-1Q role, BuNo 147865 was used as an aerodynamic prototype, and A2F-1 BuNo 148618 was used as the electronic prototype. 148618 flew for the first time on April 26 and the most significant external change was the presence of a canoe-shaped fin-tip fairing to accommodate a set of antennae for a Bunker-Ramo ALQ-86 receiver/surveillance system. This system included AN/ALQ-41, AN/ALQ-51, and AN/ALQ-55 jamming systems and its primary mission was to suppress enemy electronic activity during air strikes. In addition, the aircraft could

carry up to five jammer pods on underwing pylons and on the centreline. These pods included the AN/ALQ-31B, AN/ALQ-54, or AN/ALQ-76, and chaff dispensers (either AN/ALE-32 or AN/ALE-41) could be substituted for the underwing jammer pods. The aircraft retained a limited all-weather attack capability, although EA-6As were very seldom used for offensive operations. The aircraft could carry and launch the AGM-45 Shrike missile, but this was very rarely used operationally.

Only twenty-seven EA-6As were built, (two prototypes, ten modified from A-6A airframes, plus fifteen production aircraft built from scratch as EA-6As). These aircraft served with the US Marine Corps in Vietnam as supplements and later replacements for the EF-10B (F3D-2Q) Skyknights. The first operational aircraft were delivered to VMCJ-1 at MCAS Cherry Point, North Carolina on December 1, 1965. The EA-6As were first deployed to Southeast Asia in October of 1966 and the first twelve aircraft were equipped with the AN/ALQ-53 ECM system, plus an AN/ALR-15 radar warning receiver. On the fifteen purpose-built EA-6As, the AN/ALQ-86 surveillance receiver system and the AN/ALQ-76 jamming systems replaced the earlier systems.

The purpose-built EA-6As were distributed to three operational Marine Corps squadrons VMCJ-1, -2, and -3 and the aircraft served

EA-6A 151599 of VAQ-33.

One of the EA-6As
that served in
Vietnam

A grey clad EA-6A 151598/AF prepares to launch.

EA-6A 148618/CY
with the famous
'Playboy Bunny'
tail emblem

Where all old
aircraft go to die –
Davis Monthan's
Boneyard

EA-6A 151599 shown later in its career in low visibility grey

An unidentified EA-6A moves into position on the deck

EA-6A 149475/GD of VAQ-33

along RF-4B Phantoms in VMCJ-1, -2, -3 until 1975, when a decision was made to separate the two types into different squadrons. All of the EA-6As were moved into VMA-1, and some were later given to the Reserve squadron VMAQ-4. These units later transitioned to the EA-6B, and their EA-6As were issued to Navy squadrons VAQ-33, VAQ-209, and VAQ-309. In 1985, the EA-6As were upgraded by replacing the ALQ-41 with the ALQ-126B, the addition of a new radar warning receiver, and the improvement of several systems. In later years, the EA-6As remaining in service were used primarily for training and for testing of friendly air defences. The Marine Corps finally retired their last EA-6A in 1985, and although the Navy never used the EA-6A in active-duty squadrons, several Marine Corps detachments deployed aboard Navy carriers in the Mediterranean and the Western Pacific in the early 1970s, and in 1981 a Marine Corps reserve squadron was activated with EA-6As. The last EA-6A left Navy service in October 1993, when VAQ-33 was disestablished. ▣

A classic shot showing the A-6 Intruder heritage.

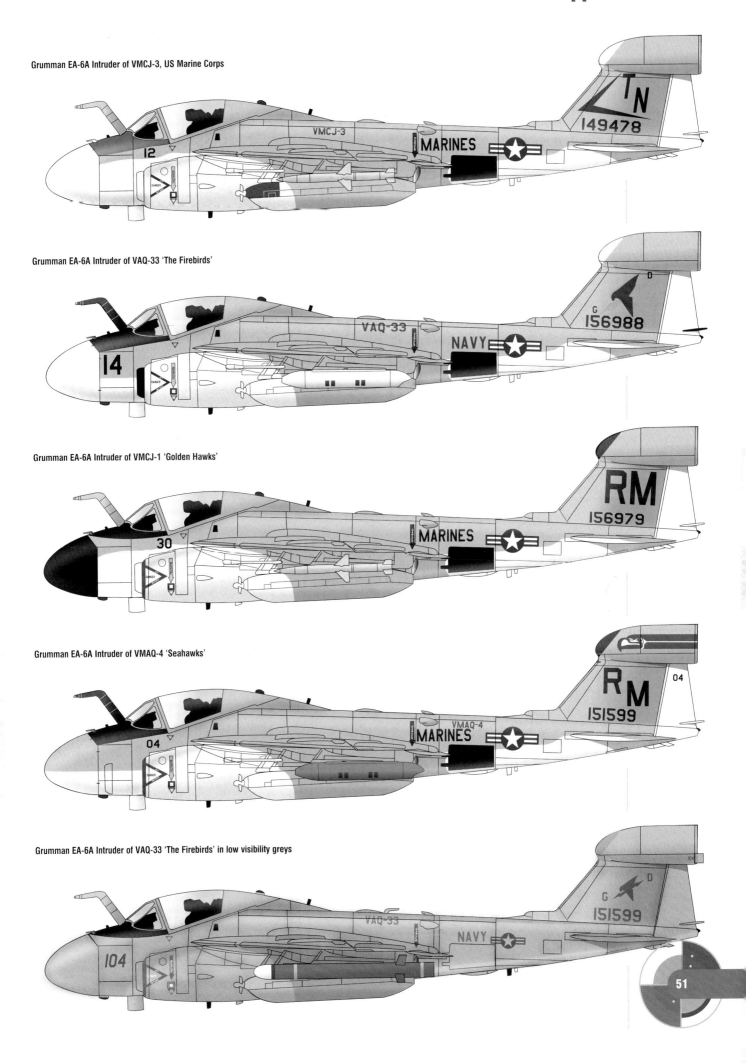

Grumman EA-6A Intruder of VMCJ-3, US Marine Corps

Grumman EA-6A Intruder of VAQ-33 'The Firebirds'

Grumman EA-6A Intruder of VMCJ-1 'Golden Hawks'

Grumman EA-6A Intruder of VMAQ-4 'Seahawks'

Grumman EA-6A Intruder of VAQ-33 'The Firebirds' in low visibility greys

On the Prowl
The EA-6B Prowler
The US Navy and Marine Corps 'tron-fighter'

The EA-6B Prowler is a vital airborne asset and is included in every aircraft carrier deployment, with a unique primary mission - to protect fleet surface units and other aircraft by jamming hostile radars and communications. As a result of restructuring US assets in 1995, the EF-111 Raven was retired, leaving the EA-6B as the only radar jammer in the US inventory, and as such five new squadrons were stood up, four of which are dedicated to supporting USAF Expeditionary Force wings.

The heart of the EA-6B is the AN/ALQ-99 Tactical Jamming System. The Prowler can carry up to five pods (one belly mounted and two on each wing) and each pod is integrally powered and houses two jamming transmitters that cover one of seven frequency bands. The EA-6B can carry any mix of pods, fuel tanks and/or HARM anti-radiation missiles depending on mission requirements. The EA-6B's tail fin pod or 'football' houses sensitive surveillance receivers, capable of detecting hostile radar emissions at long range and emitter information is processed by a central mission computer. Detection, identification, direction-finding, and jammer-set-on-sequence can all be performed automatically or by the crew, which consists of a pilot and three electronic countermeasures officers (ECMOs). The ALQ-99 jammers are operated by the two ECMOs in the aft cockpit, whilst the ECMO in the right front seat is responsible for navigation, communications, and defensive electronic countermeasures. The EA-6B's ALQ-99 is used to collect tactical electronic order of battle (EOB) data, which can be recorded and processed after missions to provide updates to various orders of battle. The ALQ-00 TJS is used to provide active radar jamming support to assault support and attack aircraft, as well as ground units.

The Prowler is not optimised to provide an electronic 'safe haven', but if used efficiently and effectively, the EA-6B can provide a decisive tactical advantage. Whether the crew of four is assigned to a carrier-based Navy VAQ squadron, Marine Corps VMAQ squadron, or a newly formed, jointly manned Navy land-based squadron (also VAQ) they come as a highly standardised crew, able to work with any mix or strike

package. The Prowler fleet continues to be modernised and upgraded to keep the aircraft and its systems abreast of evolving threats, and to maintain aircraft safety. In March 2001 the Navy and Marine Corps had three configurations of ICAP II EA-6B aircraft, the Block 82, Block 89, and Block 89A. The EA-6B ICAP II Block 89 aircraft has replaced the EA-6A in the Navy Reserve and the Block 89A upgrade program will bring eighty-nine of the 123 EA-6B aircraft, including all Block 82 aircraft, into a single avionics configuration for upgrade to the ICAP III. The remaining thirty-four EA-6B Block 89 aircraft will upgrade directly to ICAP III configuration.

Upward hingeing canopies

An EA-6B from
VMAQ-2

Flares are back it
seems!

Marine Prowlers
can also be land-
based from
prepared airfields,
as can be seen
here in Iraq

A pair of Prowlers from VAQ-139 aboard the USS John C Stennis

The Block 89A upgrade program addresses structural and supportability problems associated with aging aircraft and includes numerous avionics improvements for safety of flight and joint interoperability. Further improvements to the Prowler's AN/ALQ-99 tactical jamming system, include the Improved Capabilities (ICAP) III upgrade, new high and low frequency transmitters, and continuing structural enhancements, will ensure that the EA-6B remains the world's premier tactical electronic warfare platform and a force multiplier for years to come. ICAP III also includes a new receiver intended to provide a reactive jamming capability and includes provisions for Link 16 connectivity. The Marine Corps EA-6B Prowler also provides Airborne Command and Control (C2W) support to Fleet Marine Forces as well as electronic attack (EA), tactical electronic support (ES), electronic protection (EP) and high speed anti-radiation missile (HARM).

In a strike mission the Prowler is mainly utilised for Suppression of Enemy Air Defenses, or SEAD. The first part of an enemy's air defense system a strike package encounters is the Early Warning (EW) radars. These defence systems depend on these EW radars to indicate the direction and location of forces approaching the enemy's territory. With an EA-6B flying within a strike package and producing jamming signals, the enemy's ability to detect the approaching force is greatly reduced. Another aspect of an air defence system is SAMs. Numerous SAM systems require an electronic tracking radar system in order to be effective and when this energy illuminates friendly forces the EA-6B can fire a HARM missile which guides in on the radiated energy destroying the radar.

Whilst Navy and Marines Prowlers operate from on board aircraft carriers, Marine Prowlers can also be land-based from prepared airfields, or they can operate from expeditionary airfields (EAF). They may also be sea-based, operating from aircraft carriers. Marine Prowlers are unique in their integration with the Tactical Electronic Processing and Evaluation System (TERPES). TERPES provides post-mission analysis of EA-6B ES data for reporting and updating orders of battle. The EA-6B will begin retirement in 2010, after a career that exceeded over forty-years of deployments in support of USN, USMC, and USAF and NATO strike forces. As of early 2000, the Defense Department was planning a replacement for the EA-6B Prowler and settled on a version of the ubiquitous Hornet the EA-18 'Growler' which is an F/A-18E/F modified for escort and close-in jamming.

You get a great impression of the imposing size of the Prowler here

'Prowler Power', an EA-6B gets airborne

55

EA-18G 'Growler'
Super-Bug Zappers
The plastic prowler

Undertaking carrier trials

The EA-18G Growler aircraft is a derivative of the F/A-18F Super Hornet with structural changes and the installation of new avionics and mission systems, increasing for the electronic warfare mission. One of the most visible external characteristics is that wingtip air-to-air missiles on the F/A-18 Super Hornet have been replaced by wideband receiver pods and the other hardpoints can carry a mix of electronic warfare pods and weapons. The Growler aircraft has eleven stations for carrying electronic mission systems and weapons and can also be used to carry out conventional strike missions when the requirement for EA and SEAD is reduced.

The Growler's first test flight was successfully completed in August 2006 and this was followed by delivery of the first two test aircraft in September and November 2006 and the first production aircraft was delivered to the Navy in September 2007. The first operational aircraft was delivered to NAS Whidbey Island in June 2008 and operational evaluation began in October 2008 aboard the USS John C Stennis. When the evaluation program concluded the first of ten electronic attack squadrons VAQ-129 'Vikings' stood up at NAS Whidbey Island, on 3 June 2008 to begin EA-18G operations. Deliveries of 88 Growler aircraft are planned to conclude in 2013 and these will equip eleven squadrons, all based at Naval Air Station Whidbey Island, Washington.

The two-seat cockpit has the pilot crew station and the electronic warfare officer's advanced crew station. The advanced crew station is equipped with a touch-screen liquid crystal display (LCD) mission systems control and display, a 203mm x 23mm full-colour tactical

LCD, and two multipurpose 127mm x 127mm LCDs. The displays have tactical aircraft moving map capability. The aircraft is equipped with HOTAS and full digital fly-by-wire controls. The aircraft is also fitted with a helmet-mounted cueing system to provide a 'first look, first shot' capability.

The EA-18G developed and manufactured by Northrop Grumman, has many of the advanced sensors and communications systems installed on the F/A-18 Super Hornet aircraft. The block 1 Growler is fitted with up to three AN/ALQ-99 radar jamming pods, together with an AN/ALQ-218(V)2 receiver and a Raytheon AN/ALQ-227 communications countermeasures system, both of which are mounted in the aircraft's gun bay. The AN/ALQ-99 receivers are

Resplendent in its new livery a VAQ-129 'Viking' shows off its plumage

The Growler can carry HARM missiles

installed in the tail of the aircraft and the AN/ALQ-99 pod houses the exciters and the high radiated power jamming transmitters. The block 2 Growler is equipped with the APG-79 multi-mode radar with passive detection mode and active radar suppression, ALQ-218(V)2 digital radar warning receiver and ALE-47 countermeasures dispenser.

The advanced tactical radar, the APG-79 Active Electronically Scanned Array (AESA) radar, provides air-to-air and air-to-ground capability with detection, targeting, tracking and protection modes. The AN/ALQ-218(V)2 is a variant of the Improved Capabilities (ICAP) III system deployed on the US Navy's EA-6B Prowler aircraft and the system's antennas are located on the port and starboard sides

of the nose, the engine bays, in the wingtip pods and to the aft of the cockpit, providing 360° azimuthal cover. The aircraft is armed with the AIM-120 AMRAAM advanced medium-range air-to-air missiles and AGM-88 HARM high-speed anti-radiation missiles and ALE-47 countermeasures dispensers

In a surveillance-only configuration the Growler can be armed with two AIM-120 air-to-air missiles for self defence, and for stand-off jamming and escort jamming missions the Growler can be armed with two AGM-88 HARM missiles plus two AIM-120 AMRAAMs. In a strike configuration the Growler can be armed with two AGM-88 HARM missiles, two AGM-154 JSOW Joint Stand-Off Weapon (block 2 aircraft) and AIM-120 AMRAAMs. **C5**

Down safely…..

600

600N

Vortices stream from
the propeller tips as
this Hawkeye takes off

Eyes of the Fleet
The E-2C Hawkeye
Grumman's Mini-AWACS

The Grumman E-2 Hawkeye is an all-weather, carrier-capable Airborne Early Warning (AEW) aircraft, primarily used by the US Navy. This twin-turboprop was designed and developed during the late 1950s and early 1960s as a replacement for the E-1 Tracer, which was rapidly becoming obsolete. The E-2 performance has since been upgraded with the E-2B, and E-2C versions, where most of the changes were made to the radar and communications suite, and the fourth version of the Hawkeye is the E-2D, which first flew in 2007. The E-2 also received the nickname 'Super Fudd' as it replaced the E-1 Tracer 'Willy Fudd' and in recent times it has been commonly referred to as the 'Hummer' because of the distinctive sounds of its turboprop engines.

In US service, the E-2 Hawkeye provides all-weather AEW and Command and Control capabilities for Navy battle-groups and in addition, its other purposes include sea and land surveillance, the control of strike aircraft on offensive missions, and the control of search and rescue missions. The original E-2C, known as the Group

0, became operational in 1973, and it has undergone several upgrade programs during the decades since. The first of these was the E-2C Group I which replaced the E-2's older APS-125 radar and T56-A-425 turboprops with their improvements, their APS-139 radar systems and T56-A-427 turboprops. This version of the E-2 was followed within a few years by the more-improved Group II of the E-2C, which had the better APS-145 radar. The Group II has been incrementally upgraded with new navigational systems, better situational displays, and computerized electronics, culminating in the E-2C Hawkeye 2000 variant (sometimes called the Group III, although this term is no longer used as an official designation).

The E-2C and E-2D Hawkeyes use advanced electronic sensors, especially its radars that can now provide better early warning of enemy aircraft and anti-ship missile attacks. The Hawkeye 2000 features the APS-145 radar with a new mission computer and CIC (Combat Information Centre) workstations and carries the Navy's new CEC (cooperative engagement capability system. Although once

An E-2C comes in to land

59

Crew ensure the aircraft is secured on the catapult track

The 'shooter' says… 'Go'!

A rare sight – E-2's in formation!

The E-2C and E-2D
Hawkeyes use advanced
clcotronic sensors

61

A superb shot of an E-2 assigned to the USS Kitty Hawk

considered for replacement by the Common Support Aircraft, the Hawkeye will continue in its role as the Navy's primary AEW aircraft for years into the future in the E-2D version. Since entering combat in 1964 during the Vietnam War, the E-2 has served the US Navy around the world, acting as the electronic 'eyes of the fleet'. The E-2 Hawkeye is a crucial component of the US Navy Carrier Air Wings, and each carrier is equipped with four Hawkeyes (five in some

Under a veil of steam an E-2 unfolds its wings

The E-2 is the 'eyes of the fleet'

situations), allowing for continuous 24-hour-a-day operation of at least one Hawkeye, and allowing for one or two of them to be undergoing maintenance.

In the mid-1980s, several E-2Cs were bailed from the Navy to the Coast Guard and the U.S. Customs Service for counter-narcotics (CN) and maritime interdiction operations (MIO). During Operation Enduring Freedom and Iraqi Freedom all ten Navy Hawkeye squadrons flew overland sorties and provided battle management for attack of enemy ground targets, close-air-support coordination, combat search and rescue control, airspace management, as well as datalink and communication relay for both land and naval forces. Hawkeye 2000s first deployed in 2003 aboard the USS Nimitz with VAW-117, the 'Wallbangers', and now the E-2Cs have been upgraded with eight-bladed propellers as part of the NP2000 program; the first squadron to cruise with the new propellers was VAW-124 'Bear Aces'. The latest version can track more than 2,000 targets simultaneously (while at the same time, detecting 20,000 simultaneously) to a range greater than 400 mi (640 km) and simultaneously guide 40–100 air-to-air intercepts or air-to-surface engagements. ⬛

Super COD
The C-2 Greyhound
Ship-board hauler

A very colourful Greyhound!

The C-2 Greyhound is a twin-engine cargo-carrying aircraft designed to carry mail and supplies to and from US Navy aircraft carriers, under the aegis of COD – Carrier On board Delivery. The C-2 Greyhound is a derivative of the E-2 Hawkeye and as such shares the same wings and power plants, but has a widened fuselage with a rear loading ramp. The first of two prototypes flew in 1964, production began the following year and the aircraft eventually replaced the C-1 Trader in the COD role, and in 1984 the Navy ordered thirty-nine new C-2A aircraft to replace the older airframes. Dubbed the 'Reprocured' C-2A - C-2A(R) - due to the similarity to the original, the new aircraft has airframe improvements and better avionics. The older C-2As were phased out in 1987, and the last of the new models was delivered in 1990. Powered by two Allison T56 turboprop engines, the C-2A can deliver up to 10,000 pounds of cargo, passengers or both. It can also carry litter patients in medical evacuation missions. A cage system or 'transport stand' restrains cargo during carrier launch and landing and the large aft cargo ramp and door and a powered winch allow straight-in rear cargo loading and unloading for fast turnaround. Its ability to airdrop supplies and personnel, fold its wings, and generate power for engine starting and other uses provide an operational versatility found in no other cargo aircraft.

The Hawkeye lineage is apparent in the wings and tail

What it's all about – mail and parcels from home!

A dramatic shot as a
C-2 comes in to land

Having landed this C-2 cracks its wings and taxies away

A hint of burning rubber as this C-2 traps the 'wire'

The odd, quadruple-rudder is due to aircraft carrier hangar deck height restrictions so for adequate directional control of an aircraft of this size, a single rudder would have been too tall. It also places the outboard rudder surfaces directly in line with the propeller wash, providing effective yaw control even as the plane's airspeed approaches zero, as during takeoff and landing. Between November 1985 and February 1987, VR-24 and its seven 'Reprocured' C-2As demonstrated the aircraft's exceptional operational readiness as the squadron delivered 2,000,000 pounds of cargo, 2,000,000 pounds of mail and 14,000 passengers in the European and Mediterranean theatres. The C-2A(R) also served the carrier battle groups during Desert Shield, Desert Storm and Enduring Freedom

All thirty-six C-2A(R)s are undergoing a critical Service Life Extension Program (SLEP) and current plans require the C-2A to perform its mission supporting battle group operational readiness through 2015. The landing limit is quickly approaching for most of the airframes, and the SLEP will increase the Greyhound's projected life to 15,000 hours total time or 36,000 landings. Once the program is complete, it will allow the current thirty-six aircraft to operate until 2027. The SLEP includes structural improvements to the center wing, navigational upgrades including the addition of GPS and the dual CAINS II Navigation System, the addition of crash survivable flight incident recorders, and a Ground Proximity Warning System. The first upgraded C-2A(R) left NAVAIR Depot North Island on September 12, 2005, after sitting on the ground for three and a half years while the SLEP was developed and installed, and an eight-bladed NP2000 propeller is another part of this upgrade expected to be installed.

Last mail home...

The Frog
Boeing-Vertol CH-46
The Sea Knight

The Boeing CH-46 Sea Knight or 'Frog' in Navy parlance has served the US Navy and Marine Corps faithfully since the early 1960's. This now venerable aircraft's primary missions in Navy service include Combat Logistics Support, Vertical Replenishment (VERTREP), Search and Rescue, and Special Operations. As a Marine Corps platform, the H-46E is used primarily during cargo and troop transport. The unique tandem-rotor design of the Sea Knight permits increased agility and superior handling qualities in strong relative winds from all directions, allowing, in particular, rapid direction changes during low airspeed manoeuvring. This capability has resulted in the safe, efficient and graceful transfer of many millions of tons of cargo and many thousands of passengers over the years.

The H-46 Sea Knight helicopter is one of the largest helicopters in the US Navy inventory. and is a twin-turbine powered, dual-piloted, tandem rotor helicopter designed by Boeing's Vertol Division. The 'Frog' is 16 feet 8 inches tall and the six rotor blades on the aircraft each measure 25 feet 6 inches. With blades spread, the aircraft is 84 feet 4 inches long and the average weight of the H-46 is 18,000 pounds, with a maximum lift capability of 6,000 pounds. It can carry

Just how low can you go? This CH-46 is caught just above the waves on a VERTREP mission.

25 combat-loaded troops, or can be outfitted to carry medical evacuation litters in case of disaster. It has the fuel capacity to stay airborne for approximately two hours, or up to three hours with an extra internal tank. The helicopter also has the ability to land and taxi on the water in case of emergency, and is able to stay afloat for up to two hours in two-foot high seas.

During 1960, the Marines derived a requirement for a twin-turbine troop/cargo assault helicopter to replace the piston engine types then in use. Following a design competition, Boeing-Vertol was selected to build its model 107M as the HRB-1, early in 1961. Special features included power-operated blade folding, integral cargo handling provisions, a rear loading ramp that could be left open in flight, personnel recovery and rescue equipment, and provision for hoisting 10,000 pounds externally. These and other features marked a significant step forward in helicopter capability in the time period. The first flight in August 1962 was followed by a change in designation to CH-46A, development flight testing, (including the first NPE in January 1963), and BIS trials beginning in March 1964. Fleet introduction of CH-46As with the Marines and UH-46As with

the Navy took place in November 1964. The latter were modified for use in the vertical replenishment role.

The CH-46 Sea Knight was first procured in 1964 to meet the medium-lift requirements of the Marine Corps in Vietnam with a program buy of 600 aircraft. The aircraft has served the Marine Corps in all combat and peacetime environments, however, normal airframe operational and attrition rates have taken the assets to the point where a medium lift replacement is required. The safety and capability upgrades are interim measures to allow continued safe and effective operation of the Sea Knight fleet until a suitable replacement is fielded. Production continued in subsequent years, along with modifications to improve some of the H-46's characteristics. With

service in Southeast Asia came installation of guns and armour. Increased power requirements were met by installation of higher powered T58-GE-10s in the CH/UH-46D models, which also featured new cambered (droop snoot) rotor blades. The final CH-46E, with further increased power, was preceded by the last production version, the CH-46F, before production was completed with delivery of the 524th H-46 in February 1971. The early A models now serve as search and rescue HH-46As. CH-46s equip Marine Reserve squadrons, and conversion of earlier aircraft to the new CH-46E version was completed with fibreglass blades added to its other improvements.

The mission of the CH-46E Sea Knight helicopter in a Marine

A Camouflaged Marines CH-46 in action in Bosnia

VERTREP is one of the Sea Knight's primary functions.

The 'Frog' is 16 feet 8 inches tall and the six rotor blades on the aircraft each measure 25 feet 6 inches

A brace of CH-46s go about their 'business'

A line-up of 'Frogs' with their access panels open for maintenance.

Increased power requirements were met by installation of higher powered T58-GE-10 engines.

Medium Helicopter (HMM) squadron is to provide all-weather, day/night, night vision goggle (NVG) assault transport of combat troops, supplies, and equipment during amphibious and subsequent operations ashore. Troop assault is the primary function and the movement of supplies and equipment is secondary. Additional tasks are: combat and assault support for evacuation operations and other maritime special operations; over-water search and rescue augmentation; support for mobile forward refuelling and rearming points; aero medical evacuation of casualties from the field to suitable medical facilities. A new CH-46 Sea Knight Upgrade Programme has provided for an increased fuel capacity in the stub wings and an emergency helicopter flotation system. The installation of a new rotor head and upgraded transmission has improved flight and rotor controls, and eliminated constant rotor head inspections. Two additional upgrades to the 'Frog' have included the installation of an ARC-210 radio and a night vision goggle compatible heads-up display, which has been installed alongside the integrated communication navigation control system modification.

The Navy Air Systems Command ordered the grounding of all CH-46 helicopters on 18 August 2002 as a precaution after discovery of a crack in a rotor component of a Sea Knight at the Cherry Point Marine Corps Air Station in North Carolina. A similar problem was found a few days later in a CH-46 deployed aboard the amphibious assault ship Belleau Wood in the Persian Gulf area. Inspection of all 291 CH-46 Sea Knight helicopters in the Navy and Marine Corps found only one with a flaw of the kind that triggered the temporary grounding of the fleet, and the full fleet was returned to service. The Sea Knight continues to serve with distinction and has seen action in both Gulf Wars as well as operations in Afghanistan, the Balkans and various worldwide exercise commitments. Slated to be eventually replaced by the MV-22 Osprey, the Sea Knight seems set to enjoy a few years more service as the Osprey's protracted development continues. 🔲

Crew work on the sand filters fitted for desert operations

Dragon Riders!

The MH-53E

Dragon of the sea

An MH-53E Sea Dragon assigned to HM-15, tows an Mk.105 Magnetic Influence Minesweeping System during operations with the amphibious assault ship USS Saipan

MH-53E Sea Dragon is the western world's largest helicopter, and is a less well known version of the CH-53 Sea Stallion. The CH-53E/MH-53E is designated 'S-80' by its manufacturers Sikorsky, and is commonly referred to as the 'Hurricane Maker' by deck crews because of the downwash the helicopter generates. The MH-53E is used primarily for Airborne Mine Countermeasures (AMCM), with a secondary mission of shipboard delivery. Additional mission capabilities include air-to-air refuelling, hover in-flight refuelling, search and rescue, and external cargo transport operations, in both land and seaborne environments. The MH-53E is heavier and has a greater fuel capacity than the CH-53E and can operate from carriers and other warships. The Sea Dragon is capable of carrying up to fifty-five troops or a sixteen-ton payload over some fifty nautical miles, or a ten-ton payload five-hundred nautical miles. The MH-53E is capable of towing a variety of mine-sweeping countermeasures systems, including the Mk.105 minesweeping sonar, and the Mk.103 mechanical minesweeping system. ⊏⊐

You can almost feel the rotor-wash here!

The MH-53E is capable of towing a variety of mine-sweeping countermeasures systems, including the Mk 105 minesweeping sled, the ASQ-14 side-scan sonar, and the Mk.103 mechanical minesweeping system

The enormous Sea Dragon is an imposing sight!

Desert Storm

Wings over the Sand
The First Gulf War 1991

For the US Navy this meant bringing to bear the 'tip of the sword' power projection in the shape of fighter, bomber and control aircraft launched into battle from their massive aircraft carrier presence, while the US Marines, in concert with their doctrine, provided air and fire support from both land and sea. The Iraqi forces were hit with both technologically advanced weapons systems and overwhelming firepower, a double hit from which they never recovered.

An F-14 overflies one of Kuwait's burning oil wells

US Navy
F-14 Tomcat – Big Cats in the Gulf

The threat from the Iraqi Air Force was quickly negated by shore-based F-15 Eagles, although in the early days of the war there were plenty of calls for fighter sweeps to protect the inbound Naval and coalition bombers. The later Tomcats concentrated on fighter escort and reconnaissance using their TARPS (Tactical Airborne Reconnaissance Pod System) pods.

A number of aircraft within the Carrier Air Wing were specifically outfitted for TARPS missions and these sorties became of vital importance to allied commanders who relied on their pre- and post-strike imagery, as well as providing information on the hunt for Scud missiles, battlefield movements and installations.

F/A-18A/C – Stingers on Station

Numerically the largest contingent of naval aircraft came from the multi-role F-/A-18A and C model Hornet community. The beauty of the Hornet was that it could switch from ground attack to air defence all in the same mission by the flick of a switch which quickly moved its avionics from mud mover to fighter. The Hornets were also extensively used in the SEAD (Suppression of Enemy Air Defences) role carrying AGM-88 HARM anti-radar missiles.

One of the aircraft's major deficiencies was its lack of range, so most flights were undertaken with additional fuel tanks on the wings and centreline; however this shortcoming made no real difference to the outstanding contribution of the aircraft as an all-round fighter/bomber. Bomb loads in general were of the 'iron' variety with Mk 82 and Mk 84 slick munitions being carried, along with AIM-7 Sparrows on day missions along with the ever present AIM-9 Sidewinder.

An F/A-18C pumps out chaff and flares, a familiar scene to any pilot on a raid into Iraq, hoping to defeat any SAM launches against his aircraft

radar, and is also reported to have carried fire bombs, rocket pods and AGM-45 Shrike missiles.

A small number of KA-6D Intruder Tankers were also employed in the Gulf, providing a limited refuelling capability to mostly Navy aircraft.

A-7E Corsair – 'Sluff in the Gulf'
Literally on the verge of retirement from the Navy, the A-7E's swansong was both glorious and unique. Of the last remaining units, VA-37 and VA-105 were scheduled to be sent to the Gulf, however they were left to move to the Hornets and although VA-46 and VA-72 had already sent half of its crews for training on the Hornet, reclaimed their aircraft and aircrew and were re-assembled and hurriedly despatched aboard the USS John F Kennedy.

The aircraft went out in a blaze of glory, participating in the first strikes of the war and continued to ply their trade to the bitter end flying no fewer than 731 sorties, at one point launching eighteen fully loaded aircraft in one carrier cycle! They carried HARM anti-radar missiles and Walleye glide bombs as well as a normal full complement of cluster and iron bombs against Iraqi facilities. The A-7 also used an AAW-9 data link to guide SLAM missiles launched by A-6 Intruders, as well as carrying a pair of Sidewinder missiles for self protection.

EA-6B – 'Jamming'
The Prowlers supported the USAF's EF-111s in the high threat environments, and provided ECM coverage for nearly every coalition strike package, and usually included at least two or three HARM missile launches per mission. Although the aircraft were used in the 'stand-off' role, occasionally they were called upon to fly with the attack aircraft and indeed were themselves occasional targets for Iraqi AAA and SAM missiles.

E-2C Hawkeye
Working in concert with their larger cousins the E-3 AWACS, the smaller 'mini-AWACS' E-2Cs provided a solid air picture for the carrier battle groups and the command structures as a whole.

Maintainers fuss over an F/A-18C readying it for a trip into 'bandit country'

A-6E Intruder – 'Bomb Trucking'
At the time of the Gulf War the A-6E had celebrated its twenty-fifth anniversary and had been in constant use by the US Navy, and as such was the most combat-experienced in the service. However, it was now on the verge of retirement, to be replaced by the F/A-18 Hornet. The Intruders were in the thick of the action almost from the word go, and were privy to some of the most intense flak concentrations of the war. With their renowned ability to carry a heavy war load of up to twenty Rockeye CBUs, ten Mk 83 1,000lb or four 2,000lb iron bombs, the Intruders operated throughout the war carrying a variety of weaponry from the aircraft carriers USS Independence, USS Eisenhower, USS Midway, USS John F Kennedy, USS America, USS Saratoga USS Ranger and USS Theodore Roosevelt.

To aid its work the aircraft had received the target recognition/attack multi-sensor (TRAM) in a chin turret containing a forward-looking infra-red (FLIR) system and a laser designator and receiver, however, despite the fancy kit, weapons deliveries still had to be made in a stable flight, making the aircraft vulnerable to ground fire, as a few Intruders found out to their cost. 152928 from VA-155 and its crew was lost on 18 January, 155632 from VA-36 and crew was lost on 2 February to AAA, and a further aircraft from VA-35 was badly damaged but managed to get 'home'.

The A-6Es also launched SLAM (Standard Land Attack Missiles) as well as Walleye II glide bombs, and Paveway Laser Guided Bombs. Like all the naval aircraft the A-6 also carried TALD (Tactical Air Launched Decoy) at the onset of the war, designed to spoof enemy

Both Navy and
Marines Corps
flyers were grateful
to drogue-equipped
USAF Tankers like
the KC-135 during
the war

Loaded with LGBs an F/A-18C heads for Iraq

A look at some mission markings on an A-6E Intruder

S-3 Viking

With the submarine threat being non-existent some aircraft were flown ashore to make more room on the carriers. A few Vikings were used for COD (Carrier On-board Deliveries), and later found a low-key role as a long-range surveillance platform, and occasionally as a strike platform carrying bombs or Maverick missiles. Some of the Vikings were also outfitted with wing mounted 'buddy' refuelling pods in order to augment the small number of KA-6D Intruder tankers.

C-130 Hercules

Two variants of the Hercules were used in the war, the C-130F utilised to ferry supplies and the C-130Q used as a submarine communications platform.

Vital to the protection of the Carrier Air Group and coalition commanders was the E-3C Hawkeye mini-AWACS

Sea Surveillance – P-3 Orion

The P-3 Orion aircraft flew round the clock surveillance and targeting missions and Battle Damage Assessment. The more specialised EP-3 Aries flew electronic support and reconnaissance missions.

Rotary Support – Seahawks, Sea Sprites and Sea Kings and Super Stallions

The navy's helicopters provided many vital roles in the war, from 'plane guard duties, search and rescue resupply and heavy lift. In addition four HH-60 Rescue Hawks were mobilised from the Naval Air Reserve to provide Combat Search and Rescue abilities if needed.

US Marine Corps
F/A-18C – Mean Machines

Flying roughly similar mission profiles to their Navy counterparts the US Marines and their F/A-18A and C model Hornets worked closely with the allied ground troops in their close air support role. All of the Marines units were shore-based at Sheikh Isa AB in Bahrain, also undertaking SEAD and strike missions in the Kuwait theatre of operations often carrying up to four HARM Missiles as well as other ordnance. Deployed units included VMFA-212, VMFA-232, VMFA-235, VMFA-314, VMFA-333 and VMFA-451.

For the Marines strike packages were mostly self-contained with Hornets, Intruders and Prowlers each providing mutual support, however the Hornet's ability to carry air-to-air and air-to-ground weaponry in the same mission made it a great asset.

F/A-18D – Delta Eighteens

The two-seat 'swing role' F/A-18D was brand new to Marines service at the start of the war, with only one unit being fully operational, and as such the crews were itching to try their new mounts in combat. The F/A-18D, based on the two-seat F/A-18B trainer, was used exclusively in the Fast-FAC (Fast Forward Air Control) role by VMFA(AW)-121 'The Green Knights' who operated out of Sheikh Isa AB in Bahrain. The 'Delta Eighteen' carried advanced avionics, with the back-seater viewing his options on three CRT monitors and having independent weapons controls.

The aircraft also carried a 'strap-on' Loral AN/AAS-38 targeting

An image from a TARPS pod showing the excellent quality of image, and the damage inflicted on a HAS site

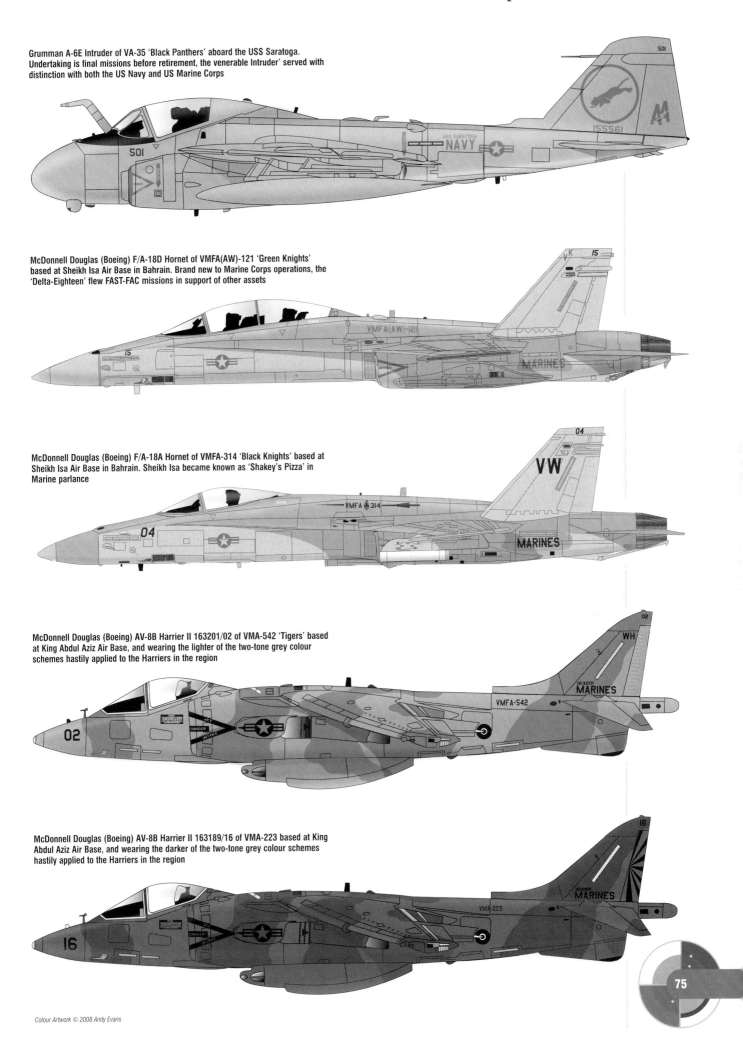

Grumman A-6E Intruder of VA-35 'Black Panthers' aboard the USS Saratoga. Undertaking is final missions before retirement, the venerable Intruder' served with distinction with both the US Navy and US Marine Corps

McDonnell Douglas (Boeing) F/A-18D Hornet of VMFA(AW)-121 'Green Knights' based at Sheikh Isa Air Base in Bahrain. Brand new to Marine Corps operations, the 'Delta-Eighteen' flew FAST-FAC missions in support of other assets

McDonnell Douglas (Boeing) F/A-18A Hornet of VMFA-314 'Black Knights' based at Sheikh Isa Air Base in Bahrain. Sheikh Isa became known as 'Shakey's Pizza' in Marine parlance

McDonnell Douglas (Boeing) AV-8B Harrier II 163201/02 of VMA-542 'Tigers' based at King Abdul Aziz Air Base, and wearing the lighter of the two-tone grey colour schemes hastily applied to the Harriers in the region

McDonnell Douglas (Boeing) AV-8B Harrier II 163189/16 of VMA-223 based at King Abdul Aziz Air Base, and wearing the darker of the two-tone grey colour schemes hastily applied to the Harriers in the region

75

Colour Artwork © 2008 Andy Evans

FLIR and a Hughes AN/AAR-50 containing a thermal imager and navigation set giving a TV quality picture in all weathers. The aircraft was also equipped with a comprehensive communications fit and a data link to pass information, such as the standard Marines 'Nine Line Briefing' directly to other aircraft or ground stations. In the nose was the AN/APG-73 multi-mode radar, capable of both air-to-air and air-to-ground modes and being able to track up to ten targets simultaneously, displaying eight to the WSO in the back.

The Hornets used their speed and systems to pick out targets, mark them with up to eight phosphorus-tipped folding-fin rockets carried in a pair of LAU-95 pods, and using their nose mounted 20mm cannon to keep any defenders' heads down. In addition, the aircraft also routinely carried a pair of trusty AIM-9 Sidewinders on their wingtips for self defence.

A-6E Intruder

Operating from Bahrain the A-6 Intruders were amongst the first Marine aircraft to be deployed to the Gulf. On the verge of retirement the 'Intruders' continued to give sterling service as medium, all-weather, 'bomb-trucks', with aircraft being drawn from VMA(AW)-224 and VMA(AW)-533, and operating in much the same pattern as their Navy counterparts.

Grumman OA-10 Bronco

Another aircraft on the verge of retirement was the OA-10 Bronco, and used in the war as an aerial observation platform to co-ordinate Marine close air support strikes against ground targets in the FAC role.

Harriers, Hornets and Cobra helicopters all benefited from the 'Bronco on station', and two versions of the aircraft were operated from Al Jubail, these being the 'vanilla' OV-10A and the FLIR

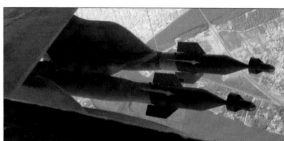

Laser Guided Bombs, such as those shown here, served with devastating effect when dropped on HAS site and other vehicles and structures

equipped OV-10D. The aircraft also sported a number of different camouflage schemes, from tactical greys to grey and green to the more eclectic two-one sand and brown.

McDonnell Douglas AV-8B – US Harriers go to war

Operation Desert Storm saw the first operational use of the second generation of Harrier, the AV-8B. This all-new aircraft was as yet untried, but was a quantum leap compared to its predecessor. The first squadrons arrived as part of 'Desert Shield' and were stationed at Sheikh Isa AB, and subsequently relocated to King Abdul Aziz Naval Base. Some Harrier operated directly from the USS Nassau, and true to Marines doctrine the aircraft also operated from a Forward Operating Location at Tanajib, just forty miles from the Kuwaiti border.

The aircraft, tasked with Close Air Support, were drawn from VMA-231, VMA-311, VMA-331 and VMA-513-Det B, and carried a wide variety of weaponry in connection with this role. Their first call to action was to aid Marines in the town of Khafji who were being shelled, and the responding aircraft quickly silenced the guns. In the early days of the war the aircraft carried a pair of AIM-9 Sidewinder missiles on their outer wing pylons, however as the war continued and the anticipated Iraqi air threat did not materialise no missiles were carried at all.

Bell AH-1W – 'Whiskey Cobras'

The Marines deployed some thirty-nine of their latest version of the ubiquitous 'Huey Cobra', the AH-1W, which to all intents and proposes flew the same mission as the Army's AH-64 Apache. They carried roughly the same armament with the Hellfire missile, although not in the same numbers, as the 'Whiskey could carry only eight of the lethal rounds whereas the Apache could carry sixteen. Other weaponry included 2.75 in Hydra rocket pods, containing high explosive fragmentation (HE-FRAG), HE Anti Tank (HEAT), Anti

Personnel (APERS) or General Purpose (GP) rounds TOW missiles (TOW, TOW-2 TOW-2A) and grenade launchers.

The AH-1W featured a pair of GE T700-GE-401 engines, chaff and flare dispensers mounted on the outsides of the stub wings and a nose-mounted M197 three-barrel 20mm cannon. The aircraft also carried a nose-mounted FLIR and laser for aiming the Hellfire missiles.

Four units were operational, HMLA-169 and HMLA-269 which were sea-based, and HMLA-367 and HMLA-369 were shore-based, whilst a further six Cobras were on loan to various units from HMLA-267. In addition to the 'Whiskey' Cobras, two Marine Reserve units HMA-773 and HMA-775 also deployed their AH-1J Sea Cobras to the Gulf.

Bell UH-1N Iroquois – Hueys in Support

Certainly one of the oldest designs employed by the US Marines was the redoubtable UH-1N 'Huey', with thirty aircraft being employed in the scout and support roles working with the Cobra attack assets.

Grumman EA-6B – Marines Prowlers

As the US Marines' only dedicated electronic warfare aircraft the 'Prowler' was in high demand to provide jamming for raids by Marines and other air assets. Their mission was much the same as the Navy EA-6Bs described earlier, although only twelve Marine Prowlers were active in the war. The aircraft, all drawn from VMAQ-2, were based at Sheikh Isa AB, and just two of their number amassed over seventy missions between them.

Lockheed KC-130 Hercules

The Hercules in Marine service was primarily involved in providing

tanker support to both deploying fighters and attack aircraft, and once in situ the Hercs continued their role then supplying aerial refuelling for strike packages. For their war role a composite unit made up of aircraft from VMGR-252 and VMGR-352 was deployed as part of Desert Shield to Bahrain, and these were followed by aircraft from VMGR-452 and VMGR-234 who deployed to Al Jubail.

Rotary Support

Once more the unsung heroes of the war were the supply and transport units of the Corps. Aircraft such as the CH-46E Sea Knight performed a variety of duties ranging from the vital movement of troops and supplies to the MedeVac missions with ten of the helo squadrons being involved. Likewise the larger CH-53A and D Sea Stallions and the CH-53E Super Stallions were heavily tasked ferrying artillery pieces around the battlefield, moving troops and flying teams to remote locations to establish FARPS.

Again some five units were involved. By far the most specialised rotary aircraft employed was the RH-53D which like its naval counterpart was employed in mine clearing operations. ▣

A Marine Corps AV-8B Harrier overflies the burning oil fields of Kuwait

The KC-130 Tanker/Transport awaits its turn on the runway as an F/A-18 comes in to land

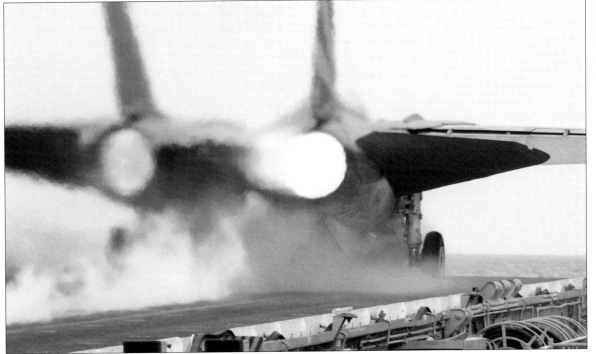

Huge plumes of flame erupt from the back end of an F-14 Tomcat as it is hurled into the air for a Combat Air Patrol mission

Shock & Awe
Operation Iraqi Freedom
Back to the Gulf again

Following just over a decade of posturing, devious diplomacy, intransigence and sabre rattling from Sadaam Hussein, the now infamous 'Weapons of Mass Destruction' allegations, and the increasing threat of global terrorism following 9-11, the international community, or more pointedly the US and UK finally served notice on the Iraqi government that they faced a campaign of 'Shock and Awe' if they did not accede to requirements of the UN Weapons inspectors and restore full co-operation and ceased any military aspirations.

By mid-March 2003 a coalition of forces led by the US and UK had once more amassed a huge military presence in the region with the remit to deliver a swift decisive strike to once and for all remove Sadaam Hussein from power and rid the region and indeed the world of the threat of his alleged chemical and biological weapons. Although the planned invasion did not carry the same weight internationally as the 1991 War, America, still smarting from 9-11 wanted the situation finally remedied with the toppling of the Iraqi regime.

The US was again poised to unleash its massive aerial prowess from both land and sea, with an array of smart and conventional weaponry available to them. Once again the old and the new were mixed, with the venerable B-52 being partnered by the B-2 and the B-1, and the F-18F Super Hornet partnered by the soon to be retired F-14 Tomcat. New weapons such as the Joint Direct Attack Munition – JDAM, CBU-105 Wind Corrected Munitions Dispenser were used in concert with more traditional iron bombs and precision guided weapons were the order of the day to facilitate the least amount of 'collateral damage' as possible.

At 5.34 local time on the 20 March 2003, aircraft and cruise missiles launched the first attacks on targets in and around Baghdad and Operation Iraqi Freedom, or 'OIF' as the Americans called it, was under way. The coalition forces struck as command and communications positions, power stations and part headquarters. Whilst the majority of attacks were carried out from bases in the region or aircraft carrier in the gulf, the 'heavy' bombers operated from bases in the UK, the Indian Ocean and continental US. The B-2s flew 34 hour long-range missions from their home at Whiteman AFB, whilst the B-52s operated from such bases as RAF Fairford in the UK and Diego Garcia. Indeed it was quite surreal to see 'live' TV news feeds from cameras overlooking the fences at Fairford as convoys of bombs were routed along the taxi-ways to the waiting B-52s! Obviously a 'cunning plan' in the hopes that other news sources would pick up on the story and warn the Iraqi populace what was en-route to them care of Uncle Sam! OIF was also the first time that all three American 'heavies', the B-1, B-2 and B-52 were involved in action, and indeed a notable first was

OIF was the only recent combat arena where Navy aircraft operated from land bases as well as carriers

A 'Black Lions' F-14D

the joint mission involving all three types where they each dropped GPS aimed bombs on a single target. Imagine being on the receiving end of that!!!

The war began with an unfortunate incident on 23 March when an RAF Tornado was shot down accidentally by the hitherto well respected US Patriot missile system which had already downed a brace of Scud missiles launched against allied bases. Like Desert Storm the US warplanes were decorated with artwork, however, much of this was lost once the aircraft retuned to their home bases. For those keen on this adornment we can heartily recommended Greg L Davies book 'Shock and Awe' published by TwoBobs Graphics which captures much of this artwork for posterity.

An F/A-18 Super Hornet of VFA-41 'Black Aces'

A good view of the increased wing area of the Super Hornet

An F/A-18F Super Hornet back aboard the Nimitz

A camouflaged F/A-18C gets airborne

Tomcat's 'Last Hurrah' F-14

The US Navy and Marines brought their own brand of power projection to the region with carriers such as the Harry S Truman, Theodore Roosevelt, Constellation, Kitty Hawk, Abraham Lincoln and later the Nimitz (replacing the Lincoln). On board Tomcats, Hornets, Prowlers and Harriers were arranged against Iraq, and for the mighty F-14 it was to be the last great war-cry of its illustrious career. Like the USAF, the employment of smart weapons was now at the fore with JDAM, JSOW and LGBs the order of the day. Having spent most of its life as a potent interceptor, the F-14 had been transformed in the decade between Gulf wars into a real multi-role platform, with the newest version the F-14D 'Bombcat' being the apex of this transformation. Now fitted with upgraded avionics and D04 computer software, allied to a LANTIRN designator pod the 'Cat' was now capable of designating its own bombs or buddy lasing for other aircraft. In addition other Tomcats were outfitted with the TARPS recce pod and thus within the 'total picture' enabled them to undertake FAC-A, SCAR, and of course Interception and Strike missions – making the aging Tomcat a far different prospect from its earlier incarnations! An F-14D from VF-2 'Bounty Hunters' became the first Tomcat unit to drop a JDAM on February 28, whilst VF-31

and VF-213 had similar success with their Tomcats, those of VF-32 aboard the Truman had their F-14Bs hastily JDAM modified prior to deployment, whereas the F-14As of VF-154 remained restricted to LGB operations only. The Tomcats worked by both night and day, with VF-2 and VF-213 being the 'night specialists, with so called 'Vampire' missions! Also of note was the shore basing of some Tomcats at Al Udeid making this the first time in recent conflict history the US Navy had flown from both land and sea simultaneously.

Sting of the Hornet - F/A-18C/E/F

In some quarters the Hornets became known as the 'Universal Soldiers' of both the Navy and Marines, and OIF saw the combat debut of the newest aircraft in the Navy's inventory, the F/A-18E single-seat and F/A-18F two-seat 'Super Hornet'. The 'Eagles' of VF-115 and their F/A-18Es were quick to showcase the talents of the new Hornet, with its increased fuel load and greater ordnance capabilities, and these jets were hotly followed by F/A-18Fs from VFA-41, VFA-14, all undertaking combat missions. VF-41 also brought into action the new SHARP (Shared Airborne Reconnaissance Pod) and the very latest ATFLIR (Advanced Tactical Forward-Looking Infra Red) as well as the JHMCS

With targeting pod in place an F-14 Bombcat in full flow

As the nose says 'Give 'em Hell!'

A pair of 'Stingers' prepares for take-off

A crewman checks out a Maverick missile on a radar equipped AV8-B II+

81

A pair of 'Rams'
at Al Jaber

The Navy and Marines heavy haulers played an important transport role

(Joint Helmet Mounted Cueing System). The bulk of the Hornets in theatre were the older 'C' models or upgraded 'A+' versions but still hugely capable and deadly bomb-trucks or fighters, and indeed the Hornets were also called in to strafe ground targets!

Prowlers on station EA-6B

The 'Prowlers' were amongst the busiest aircraft of the conflict as their dedicated jamming and defence suppression abilities were at the forefront of any strike mission, and it is a testament to them that not a single coalition aircraft fell to radar guided SAMs or AAA. Carrying HARM missiles the Prowlers could be called in to attack enemy radar sites in short order as part of their patrol or strike coverage and in terms of suppression the EA-6B's latest USQ-113 GENEX decoy jammers also allowed the aircraft to disable even small communications equipment such as mobile phones! The US Marine Corps also deployed its Prowlers to work alongside its Navy brethren, shore basing their assets at Al Jaber

Viking Valedictory

On a smaller note the S-3 Viking, which without an over surface threat saw itself without a real task, apart for short-range buddy taker missions, was given a limited attack capability and an S-3B from VS-38 fired a laser guided Maverick, designated by an F/A-18C against an Iraqi target, making this the first time in the aircraft's 30-year history that they had attacked a land-based target and the first use of a laser guided missile.

Also worthy of note was the work undertaken by the E-2C Hawkeye 'Mini-AWACS, and the SH-60 helicopters, who undertook valuable service. The Navy's (Special Operations Warfare) unit HCS-5 'Firehawks' employed its HH-60F helicopters in Baghdad and the newest of the Seahawk family the MH-60S also made its combat debut. Likewise the Navy and Marines heavy haulers in the shape of the CH-53 Sea Stallions and the MH-53 Sea Dragons provided in-theatre transport, whilst the CH-46 Sea Knights worked tirelessly transporting troops and material, as well as replenishing ships around the fleet

A Marines C-130 Hercules, one of the many transports in theatre

Harriers in action - AV-8B Night Attack and II+

The Marines aviation wing played a crucial role in OIF and saw the largest assembly of an amphibious force since WWII with the assault ships USS Tarawa, Bonhomme Richard, Kearsage, Bataan, Saipan and Boxer all involved. With their fast jets embarked on Navy carriers or land based the AV-8B Harriers provided not only firepower from the sea, but also joined their F/A-18s on land. The Marines had now phased out their vulnerable Desert Storm 'day attack' Harriers, and replaced them the night capable FLIR equipped AV-8B 'Night Attack' version or the 'II+' radar and FLIR variant. The Harriers were in action right from the start of the campaign attacking Republican Guard positions and dropping PGMs using their Litening designator pods. The Harrier provided commanders with a full 24-hour service, operating from not only the assault ships, but forward operating bases close to the front lines as well as in some instances desert roads!

Marines Stingers – F/A-18C/D Hornet

The US Marines brought ashore elements from VMFA(AW)-121 and 533 flying the F/A-18D, and VMFA-225, 232 and, 251 to Al Jaber, flying the F/A-18C and undertaking all-weather attack missions in support of coalition forces, in the same manner as those from the US Navy's Hornet units.

Marines Rotary Support

As in Desert Storm the Marines brought with them their trusted AH-1W Cobra attack helicopters armed with deadly Hellfire and TOW missiles, and these were ably backed up by the venerable UH-1 'Huey'. In a similar vein to other less glamorous assets, vital support was also provided by the Marines, CH-47 and CH-53 helicopters being amongst the many unsung warriors of the conflict.

One of the few Marine Corps F/A-18D 'Delta Hornet' with ATARS nose, but fully loaded for war

83

Big Stick
USS Theodore Roosevelt

USS Theodore Roosevelt (CVN 71) anchored in the Solent during April this year. The sheer size of the carrier, which boasts a flight deck of 1,092 feet and a height, (keel to mast top), of some 244 feet, is simply staggering. With more than 5,500 crew members aboard, many of whom were keen to go sightseeing, for a few days at least, Portsmouth became an impromptu little piece of America!

A rriving off the coast off Stokes Bay, Gosport over the weekend of 4 April 2009, on its homeward leg back to Norfolk, Virginia, the USS Theodore Roosevelt (TR) complete with Carrier Air Wing 8 (CVW-8) aboard, was impossible to miss in the Solent. The 'TR' is a relatively new ship within the Nimitz-class aircraft carrier class, having been commissioned on 25 October 1986.

For one type in particular this was possibly the last chance to see USN EA-6B Prowlers in the UK, as for one of the squadrons aboard, Electronic Attack Squadron VAQ-141 'Shadowhawks' this was to be their last cruise with their venerable 40-year-old EA-6Bs. Upon arriving back at Naval Air Station Whidbey Island, Washington State, they will begin transition to the EA-18G Growler, a specialised two-seat Electronic Warfare (EW) development of the Super Hornet.

Perhaps it's simply a sign of the times, but a USN carrier's flight deck is now dominated by the Super Hornet, and whilst the fifty-eight or so aircraft aboard during the port visit was impressive, that number was divided over only four fixed-wing types: a variety of F/A-18s (ie A+, E, F), EA-6Bs, C-2As and E-2Cs. There was also a selection of SH-60F and HH-60H Seahawks. A listing of CVW-8's squadrons is seen below.

An F/A-18C Hornet belonging to VFA-15 'Valions' was assigned to the Carrier Air Group (CAG)'s Hornet, hence the extra splash of colour and the relatively clean condition. The term CAG is still used as a nickname for the Air Wing Commander, although officially it has been changed to CVW (Carrier Air Wing using the 'V' from the carrier's designation). Note the additional artwork to the centre-line drop tank.

CVW-8's complement:

● VFA-31, AJ-100 – F/A-18E
● VFA-213, AJ-100 – F/A-18F
● VFA-15, AJ-300 – F/A-18C
● VFA-87, AJ-400 – F/A-18A+
● VAQ-141, AJ-500 – EA-6B
● VAW-124, AJ-600 – E-2C
● HS-3, AJ-610 – SH-60F/HH-60H

Not aboard: were two C-2A Greyhounds from VRC-40 Detachment 1, and one E-2C Hawkeye 2000 from VAW-124, which were deployed to RAF Lyneham during the port visit. CS

The helicopter complement aboard 'TR' was the responsibility of Helicopter Anti-submarine Squadron (HS-3) also known as the 'Tridents'. The Tridents' main mission is anti-submarine warfare, where the Seahawks are seen as 'the eyes and ears' of the 'TR' whilst at sea. However during this cruise their missions also involved providing helicopter support for a number of ground operations and intercepting suspect vessels in the Gulf.

Seen from above, the Hawkeye 2000 when in a stowed configuration will test any modeller's skills to the limit, but for those up for the challenge this view should help. Note the slight displacement of the flaps when the wings are folded.

The 'Shadowhawks Carrier Air Group (CAG)'s EA-6B wore this impressive scheme complete with a full colour 'Hawk' design on its tail. Others in the squadron wore this in subdued grey colour.

One of the most eye-catching aircraft aboard was this F/A-18E belonging to the Deputy Carrier Air Group (DCAG) Commander of VFA-31 known as the 'Tomcatters'. The squadron's emblem is the famous cartoon character 'Felix the Cat', running with a spherical bomb with a lit fuse, which can just be seen on the tails of the Hornets.

Tip of the Spear #1
Flying from the Starship
CVW-1 on board the USS Enterprise

With a floating aviation armada larger than many of the world's air arms, the United States Navy is a formidable force.

Carrier Air Wing One - CVW-1 'First and Foremost' is home based at NAS Oceana and currently assigned to the aircraft carrier USS Enterprise, CVN 65, and has been in commission longer than any other Navy air wing. Since commissioning on 1 July 1938, CVW-1 has served aboard twenty different aircraft carriers, and was originally known as the 'Ranger Air Group', serving aboard USS Ranger during the early years of carrier aviation. The air wing also operated aboard the USS Langley, the USS Saratoga and the USS Lexington, which were also in service at that time. From the beginning of World War II, and until 1943, the air wing participated in the North Africa Campaign and operated in all parts of the Atlantic and Pacific theatres. The air wing also saw action against Japan from the Philippines to Tokyo, earning two Presidential Unit Citations as well as spawning many Naval Aviation heroes.

From 1946 to 1957, CVW-1 served aboard nine different carriers, including the first Super Carrier, the USS Forrestal during the 1956-57 Suez Crisis. Between June 1966 and February 1967, CVW-1 conducted combat operations off the coast of Vietnam aboard the USS Franklin D Roosevelt and whilst on board the USS John F

Kennedy in 1975 it introduced the Navy's newest and perhaps most iconic tactical aircraft, the F-14A Tomcat, into service and at the same time took on board the S-3A Viking.

CVW-1 was assigned to the USS America in mid-1982, forming an unbreakable partnership, which finally ended with the ship's decommissioning in August 1996. During that time, the USS America/CVW-1 team conducted combat operations during the attack on Libya in 1986 and was the only carrier battle group to launch strikes in support of Operation Desert Shield and Operation Desert Storm from both the Red Sea and Persian Gulf.

With the USS America's decommissioning in August 1996, the air wing joined the USS George Washington's battle group, returning from the first deployment of a two-year association with 'The Big Stick' on 3 April 1998. Following that CVW-1 returned to USS John F Kennedy after a twenty-four year absence, deploying to the Mediterranean Sea and Persian Gulf. The air wing recently joined the USS Enterprise in May 2010 after the ship had spent more than two years in the Northrop Grumman Newport News Shipyard making sure she was ready for her 21st deployment.

Currently Carrier Air Wing One has eight squadrons assigned: VRC-40 Rawhides flying the C-2A Greyhound COD.

A 'Fighting Checkmates' Super Hornet comes aboard the Enterprise

The USS Enterprise in full flow

VMFA-251 operate the 'legacy' F/A-18C

A single US Marine Corps unit is attached to the Enterprise and here an example from VMFA-251 lights the 'cans' for take-off

The 'eyes' of the battle group is the E-2 Hawkeye and here we see an example from VAW-123 preparing to unfold its wings

The vital air-bridge between ship and shore is undertaken by the Carrier On-board Delivery attributes of the C-2A Greyhounds of VRC-40

An EA-6 ready to go

An E-2C takes the wire at the conclusion of another sortie

A Super Hornet from VFA-11 comes in to take the wire

HS-11 Dragon
Slayers flying the
SH-60F Seahawk

VAQ-137 Rooks flying
the EA-6B Prowler

VAW-123 Screwtops
flying the E-2C
Hawkeye

VFA-11 Red Rippers
flying the F/A-18F
Super Hornet

VFA-136 Knighthawks
flying the F/A-18E
Super Hornet

VFA-211 Fighting
Checkmates flying the
F/A-18F Super Hornet

VMFA-251
Thunderbolts
flying the F/A-18C
Hornet

VRC-40 Rawhides
flying the C-2A
Greyhound COD

Boeing F/A-18F Super Hornet 168916/AB
of VFA-211 Fighting Checkmates

Boeing F/A-18E Super Hornet 166822/AB
of VFA-136 Knighthawks

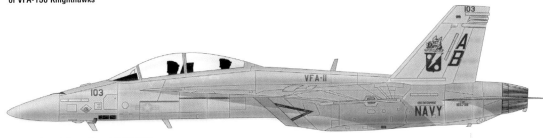

Boeing F/A-18F Super Hornet 165798/AB
of VF-11 Red Rippers

Boeing F/A-18C Hornet 164590/AB of
VMFA-251 Thunderbolts

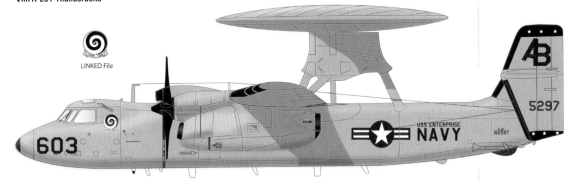

Grumman E-2C Hawkeye 162597/AB of
VAW-123 Screwtops

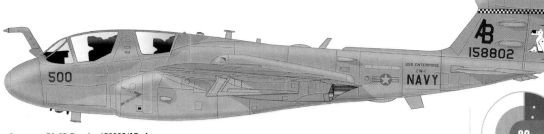

Grumman EA-6B Prowler 158802/AB of
VAQ-137 Rooks

Tip of the Spear #2
USS Dwight D. Eisenhower
On board with CVW-7

The Wildcats' CAG bird – always a colourful sight

Deck crews marshal a VAQ-140 Prowler on to the cat track

In the second of this series we take a further look at the Squadrons based on these seaborne airfields and their colours and markings.

Carrier Air Wing Seven - CVW-7 - is home based at NAS Oceana and currently attached to the USS Dwight D Eisenhower, CVN 69. Carrier Air Wing Seven was originally commissioned 20 July 1943 at NAS Alameda as Carrier Air Group Eighteen and after an intensive training period, they embarked on the USS Intrepid CV 11 and participated in combat operations against the Japanese during World War II. In September 1945, the air group transferred to NAS Quonset Point and became Carrier Air Group Seven.

During the Korean War, the air wing flew close air support strikes, attacks on industrial facilities and supply line interdiction missions from the deck of USS Bon Homme Richard. On 1 March 1978, Air Wing Seven became permanently assigned to USS Dwight D Eisenhower and deployed in January 1979 on 'Ike's' maiden voyage. From April through December 1980, the air wing embarked for an Indian Ocean deployment in support of operations to rescue the hostages in Tehran and was also on hand in 1990 to deter any Iraqi aggression as part of Operation Desert Shield and then Desert Storm.

In September 1992 CVW-7 embarked aboard the USS George Washington for a weapons system shakedown and proceeded to the Adriatic to conduct operations in support of Operation Deny Flight and Sharp Guard, following which, and in response to further

Amidst the steam from the shuttle return this F/A-18C from the Rampagers awaits its cat-shot

Deck crew prepare to launch a 'Wildcat'

Eye in the sky. A VAW-121 E-2C Hawkeye hurtles down the deck

Sweeping in for a cargo move

aggressive Iraqi troop movements south towards Kuwait, the USS George Washington and her Battle Group returned to the Gulf for further peacekeeping operations. In 1988 CVW-7 deployed aboard the USS John C. Stennis taking part in Operation Southern Watch, and in June 1999 the air wing began preparation for their next deployment which reunited them with the USS Dwight D. Eisenhower. Further operations saw them again taking part in the air wars over the Gulf in the mid 2000's and they continue to play a major role in the area. ◧

An EA-6B waits whilst this Rawhides C-2 is marshalled into position

A crew prepare their SH-60F for flight

One gone – another to follow!

Currently Carrier Air Wing Seven has eight squadrons assigned:

HS-5 Nightdippers flying the SH-60F Seahawk

VAQ-140 Patriots flying the EA-6B Prowler

VAW-121 Bluetails flying the E-2C Hawkeye

Flying the F/A-18C Hornet

VFA-103 Jolly Rogers flying the F/A-18F Super Hornet

VFA-131 Wildcats flying the F/A-18C Hornet

VFA-143 Pukin Dogs flying the F/A-18E Super Hornet

VRC-40 Rawhaides flying the C-2 Greyhound

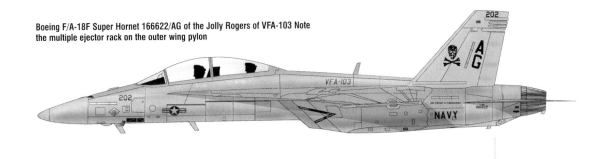

Boeing F/A-18F Super Hornet 166622/AG of the Jolly Rogers of VFA-103 Note the multiple ejector rack on the outer wing pylon

Boeing F/A-18E Super Hornet 165896/AG of the Pukin Dogs of VFA-143

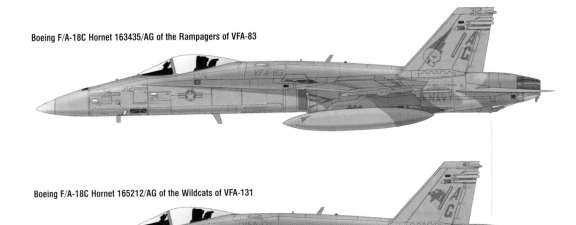

Boeing F/A-18C Hornet 163435/AG of the Rampagers of VFA-83

Boeing F/A-18C Hornet 165212/AG of the Wildcats of VFA-131

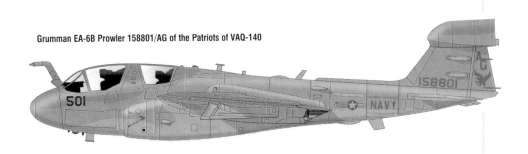

Grumman EA-6B Prowler 158801/AG of the Patriots of VAQ-140

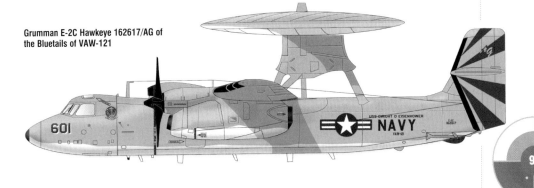

Grumman E-2C Hawkeye 162617/AG of the Bluetails of VAW-121

Tip of the Spear #3

USS Harry S Truman

At sea with CVW-3

The USS Harry S Truman (CVN 75), or 'HST' as she is commonly known, is the eighth Nimitz Class super-carrier of the United States Navy and is named after the 33rd President of the United States, Harry S Truman. 'HST's' callsign is 'Lone Warrior' and she is currently home ported at Naval Station Norfolk, Virginia. HST was launched on 13th September 1996 and was initially the flagship of Carrier Group Two and, from 1 October 2004, of Carrier Air Group Ten. The ship is 1,092 ft (333 m) long, 257 ft (78 m) wide and is as high as a twenty-four-story building, at 244 feet (74 m). The carrier can accommodate approximately eighty aircraft and has a flight deck of 4.5 acres (18,000 m²), using four elevators to move planes between the flight deck and the hangar bay. With a combat load, HST displaces almost 97,000 tons and can accommodate 6,250 crewmembers. Interestingly, the warship uses two Mark II stockless anchors that came from the USS Forrestal and is also equipped with three 20mm Phalanx CIWS mounts and two Sea Sparrow SAM launchers.

Her maiden deployment began on 28 November 2000 with Carrier Air Wing Three (CVW-3) embarked and after transiting the Suez Canal the air wing flew 869 combat sorties in support of Operation Southern Watch, including a strike on Iraqi integrated air defence system sites on 16 February 2001, in response to Iraqi SAM fire against coalition forces. These combat operations ended on 27 April and the ship returned to the US on 23 May 2001.

Her second deployment on 5 December 2002, again with CVW-3 embarked saw her air wing flying nearly 1,300 combat sorties from the Mediterranean Sea in the early stages of Operation Iraqi Freedom. ☞

A brace of F/A-18Cs from VFA-37 in tight formation

Carrier Air Wing Three (CVW-3), known as 'Battle Axe' currently has eight squadrons embarked:

VMFA-312 Checkerboards flying the F/A-18C Hornet
VFA-32 Fighting Swordsmen flying the F/A-18F Super Hornet
VFA-37 Ragin' Bulls flying the F/A-18C Hornet
VFA-105 – Gunslingers flying the F/A-18E Super Hornet

VAW-126 Seahawks flying the E-2C Hawkeye
VAQ-130 Zappers flying the EA-6B Prowler
VRC-40 Rawhides flying the C-2A Greyhound
HS-7 Dusty Dogs flying the SH-60F/HH-60F Seahawk

Steam surrounds this 'Ragin Bulls' bird as it is directed onto the cat track

Down to the hangar deck....

The USS Harry S Truman and Carrier Air Wing Three

A pair of 'stingers' on the deck elevator

The crew of this Super Hornet watch as the ordnance team prepare their bird

This E-2 bears the inscription 'Give Em Hell'

VFA-105 insignia

Boeing F/A-18E Super Hornet 166651/AC of VFA-105 Gunslingers

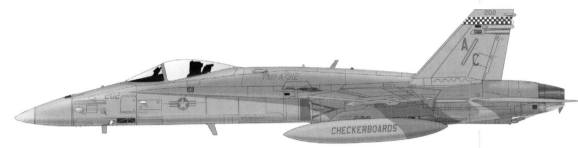

VMFA-312 insignia

Boeing F/A-18C Hornet 164909/AC of VMFA-312 Checkerboards

VFA-37 insignia

Boeing F/A-18C Hornet 165203/AC of VFA-37 Ragin Bulls

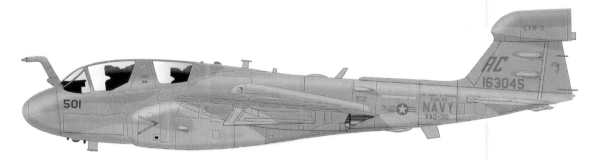

VAQ-130 insignia

Grumman EA-6B Prowler 163045/AC of VAQ-130 Zappers

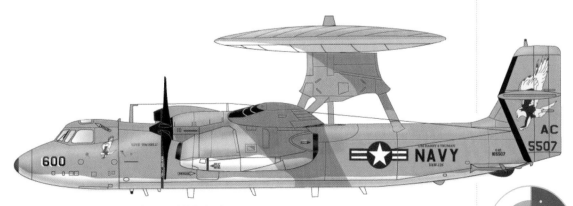

VAW-126 insignia

Grumman E-2C Hawkeye 165507/AC of VAW-126 Seahawks

SAM PUBLICATIONS

Carrier Strike
US Naval Air-Power at Sea
by Andy Evans

First produced in 2011 by SAM Limited, under licence from SAM Publications Media House, 21 Kingsway, Bedford, MK42 9BJ, United Kingdom

© 2011 SAM Publications
© Andy Evans – Text
© Andy Evans – Colour Artwork
© Vincenzo Auletta – Cover Artwork

ISBN 978-1-906959-29-6

Series Editor Andy Evans
Designed by Jonathan Phillips
Typeset by SAM Publications, Media House, 21 Kingsway, Bedford, MK42 9BJ, United Kingdom
Printed and bound in the United Kingdom by acorn web offset limited, United Kingdom

Acknowledgements
Thanks are due in no small way to the US Navy Public Affairs Department for their professional expertise in both providing information and use of many of the images that appear in this publication.

Carrier Strike is a compilation of selected articles and features, some which have previously appeared in issues of Model Aircraft Monthly, and have been expanded and enlarged, and others that have been specifically written for this publication.

The photographs that populate this work have been provided from the authors own collection, by the US Navy and via third parties from around the world. Whilst every effort has been taken to ensure the correct permissions have been obtained to use these images, the publishers cannot accept responsibility for any ommissions beyond their control. Should any persons feel their copyright has been inadvertently breached, this is wholly accidental, and in such as case please email:

andyevans@sampublications.com

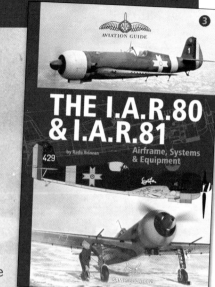